Pictures of Home

PICTURES

OF HOME

DOUGLAS BUKOWSKI

IVAN R. DEE *Chicago* 2004

PICTURES OF HOME. Copyright © 2004 by Douglas Bukowski. All rights reserved, including the right to reproduce this book or portions thereof in any form. For information, address: Ivan R. Dee, Publisher, 1332 North Halsted Street, Chicago 60622. Manufactured in the United States of America and printed on acid-free paper.

Library of Congress Cataloging-in-Publication Data:
Bukowski, Douglas, 1952–
    Pictures of home / Douglas Bukowski.
    p. cm.
    ISBN 1-56663-591-8
    1. Bukowski, Douglas 1952– 2. Polish Americans—Illinois—Chicago—Biography. 3. Chicago (Ill.)—Biography. 4. Chicago (Ill.)—Social life and customs—20th century. I. Title.

F548.9.P7B85 2004
977.3'110049185'0092—dc22
[B]

                                                    2004043847

To Bob Dietz, who served his country and loved his family

in equal measure. On Wisconsin.

Pictures of Home

Edwin

Edwin with Chester

Michael

I

STORIES

As a child I hid in my parents' bedroom closet whenever the need arose. This sanctuary was often cold, and scratchy from woolen coats that brushed against an arm or cheek. A little discomfort was the price I paid to be free of sisters and other frightful things.

The overhead shelves were another source of irritation. They hovered just out of reach, even for an enterprising boy who dragged in a dining room chair to stand on; coat sleeves always seemed to push me back. The family pictures did not move unless my mother found a reason to take them down. Finally, in adolescence, I grew tall enough to reach the shelves on my own.

At first I was drawn to the "Super Pak Snaps," palm-sized albums with Deco lettering on the cover. The "snaps" mostly show me as a baby. Only gradually did two of the background figures come into focus. They were my parents, who took or posed for pictures throughout their sixty-seven years of courtship and marriage.

The pictures are best viewed spread out across the floor or kitchen table. That way they form a snapshot chronicle of everyday life, where people and times past come back. Call it a very personal, and illustrated, history of the great South Side of Chicago, including that lace-curtain section both south and west. Hardly anyone remains of that place I come from.

Even the stray negative matters to me now. For years I kept one in a dresser drawer filled with trinkets from my life. But the silhouette refused to stay a ghost, and it took form again one Easter a few years ago. My mother and aunt each cried at the sight of their brother Charlie dressed in his work clothes for the Civilian Conservation Corps. He stands smiling on a porch somewhere, in downstate Illinois or off in California, almost two decades before he will become my godfather, just as he is now more than two decades passed. How this negative of a young man with hands on hips came into my possession I could not say.

We must have been like other families in that many, if not all, the pictures were paired with a story repeated from memory. This was how I learned about Charlie's brother, Michael. The photos show a man who gave the impression he was more comfortable around dogs than people. In one picture Michael is sitting on the living room couch at his parents' two-flat; the Sunday comics, spread over one of the cushions, did not amuse. From the expression on my uncle's face, he could have been reading the obituaries.

My mother often told how, following Pearl Harbor, Michael worried over his draft status to the point of suffering a nervous breakdown. He did not understand that the military had little interest in a truck driver already thirty-four years old. It was my father who took him to be committed so the doctors could perform a lobotomy.

Michael lived to 1989. The closest we came to meeting was the day of his funeral, when I knelt before his casket. Twelve years later, in a cedar-lined drawer at the foot of my parents' bed, I found his death certificate. There was a space to record whether the deceased ever served in the U.S. armed forces.

Somewhere is a picture of my mother's sister Lou with her husband. He caught tuberculosis in the army during World War I. They married a few years later, confident of his full recovery. But the disease consumed him anyway and sent my aunt to a city-run sanitarium. I never learned his name or that of their daughter, who died of sunstroke before she reached the age of two. The one photograph of her is badly wrinkled.

The story of my being a panicked four-year-old in a rowboat is not nearly as sad. A month before our vacation in the late summer of 1956, the *Andrea Doria* sank after colliding with another ocean liner in the Atlantic. When I saw newspaper pictures, the notion of fishing on a Wisconsin lake suddenly lost all its appeal to me. This was one of the few stories my father told about his son, and he never tired of it.

The photos do not age as much as they become strangers. Some of the very oldest pictures show my parents together with other young couples. They gather in the blush of youth now more than a half-century distant. Their obvious affection for one another all but writes the caption, friends for life. Between the three of us, my sisters and I can identify only a few of those faces. And they no longer provoke smiles of recognition from my mother.

Still other photographs assume different meanings over time. There is one in particular, of my father as a young man at a summer outing sometime in the mid-1930s. He is dressed in white pants and matching T-shirt. At six feet tall with broad shoulders, he appears every bit the sandlot football player he once was. This photo used to fill me with the envy of a son who doubted he would ever grow into the image of his father. Now I can't help but look at him and see the outlines of illness. The smile on my father's face is merely the old gridiron trick of misdirection.

The man in the picture looks to be at most thirty-three, yet he already suffered from chronic high blood pressure; it was a condition that contributed to his kidney failure in the winter of the year 2000. As to football, he played the game without a helmet because he was too much the South Side tough to bother, or he lacked the money to buy one. Either way, the decision likely affected him in the last twelve years of his life, when his brain, literally, began to shrink. A doctor told us the pounding he took as a teenager may have been a factor. It is all there in black and white.

While I don't remember being the subject of so much interest, the pictures show otherwise. There I am cradled in my father's arms, dressed to graduate from kindergarten or seated next to my sisters for a sibling portrait. My childhood was thoroughly documented if for no other reason than it could be. I have, maybe, five pictures of both my parents as children; Kodak Brownies were a hard sell to immigrant families from Galicia and Russian Poland. There is nothing of my father as an athlete and very little of him at work. So far I have run across seven such photos, and three of them were probably taken on the same day. The framed picture atop the television set may be my mother's favorite, her Edwin in his Chicago firefighter's uniform.

Growing up, I rarely, if ever, heard my father speak of his own youth. But after my thirtieth birthday he changed, and I learned to pay attention. He never let go a torrent of stories. Instead they escaped one or two at a time. My wife Michele and I might have stopped over for a visit or dinner. In passing he would tell of seeing Amelia Earhart at Municipal Airport; she had bad teeth. He also went to Detroit to see the Tigers play in the World Series, it was 1934 or '35. Oh, and he attended the air races in Cleveland around the same time. Jimmy Doolittle may have been one of the pilots.

Many other secrets my father kept to himself, like why he left school after the seventh grade. This always puzzled me, since his one brother became a dentist and the other graduated from high school. My grandmother must have decided on the middle child as breadwinner, the one male who would not die or walk out on her. But my father never said, and I never asked.

He compensated me for his silence with occasional gifts of treasure. An axe, a saw, a dairy-farm milk can and two firemen's helmets all found their way into my house, along with a large crucifix holding a gilded Christ; my father loved to pass objects through a mist of gold spray paint he conjured up in the basement. His First Communion portrait came, appropriately, in a gold frame.

The picture was taken at the Paul Studio on south Morgan Street in the neighborhood of Bridgeport, where my father grew up. His mother had decided, as other immigrant parents did, to record a child's coming of age in the church. Thus she performed the everyday miracle of the poor who find a way to pay for the necessities of life.

The studio must have charged a premium for the twenty-two-and-a-half-inch oval, hand-colored photo of her son, a handsome youth in solemn pose. There is no hint of the smart mouth that caused trouble with the police. They caught him one night playing cards on a bench in McKinley Park after curfew, and he made a wisecrack. It prompted a response which may have been delivered at the end of a billy club. I suspect the suit he wore to the studio was rented or borrowed. A small sign in front of a vase of flowers next to the Virgin Mary reads simply, 1927. My father would have been no more than fourteen.

Yet he was already working. My father worked all the time, it seemed. As a boy he helped out in the family bakery, which may be why he so freely critiqued my mother's piecrusts. When the mood struck him, he made his own. He also liked to bake and decorate the Easter Lamb cake. The cast-iron molds were from the bakery. So was the talent to apply buttercream frosting in swirls. A good decorator earned more money, he said.

My father would not have let work stand in the way of his sneaking a jelly bismarck or long john. If this constituted a vice, he was entitled. For too long his life bore the imprint of tragedies that befell his mother. Her first husband died, leaving behind two boys, and the second one ran off while she was pregnant. I did not learn about the other marriage until I was close to forty years old.

A mortgage document from 1934 lists my grandmother as divorced. Good Polish girls did not easily shed their husbands then, even those who left them. No one ever told us the name of the man or why he may have thought four months was time enough for a relationship. The divorce petition alleged that "said defendant Anton Ponicki left and abandoned" his wife on or about September 1, 1917. My father would have just turned four.

In the summer before the Great Crash, he took out a life insurance policy listing his mother as beneficiary; we found the papers after his death. The text alternates line-by-line in English and Polish. "The insured" agreed to pay a *miesięczny podatek*, or monthly assessment, of $1.19. The policy has drawings of a hospital scene and the road to happiness. This was art as motivation to keep the monthly installments coming in good times and bad. He signed the papers June 18, 1929, two months to the day before his sixteenth birthday. Eleven years later, my mother was named beneficiary.

The insurance policy coincided with my father's first real job, at the Ford assembly plant out on Torrence Avenue, where Chicago runs into the mills and refineries of northwest Indiana. On the back of his Social Security card—issued 12-19-36—are the addresses of home and factory. Today, to cover the distance between them would take close to an hour by expressway; my father depended on a series of streetcars that moved at a more leisurely pace. But he did not commute from Bridgeport. The family had already moved to what I still refer to as "my house" on Homan Avenue. Edwin Bukowski lived there for sixty-three years and six months.

The house filled with memories, not all of them easy. When his mother died in 1960, my father took to the couch in mourning because he did not know how to grieve openly in the company of others. More than twenty years passed before he called Commonwealth Edison to have his name put on the account; until then the electric bill arrived every month addressed to his mother. The Catholic missions also kept sending her mail, as if they were accustomed to receiving money orders posted from the other side.

The bungalow on Homan Avenue kept its own secrets, like the exact age of our phone number. For years my father answered calls by repeating "HEmlock 4-5574" into the receiver, assuming he did not shout "WMAQ will make me rich" to qualify for a radio contest. Everyone I knew dreaded getting him on the phone. They were intimidated by that note of challenge in his voice. It was hard to miss.

The Chicago directories do not list the Bukowski family on Homan Avenue until 1947. Either my grandmother kept an unlisted number for fear of strangers, or the house did without a phone. Either is possible. For some reason the 1946 directory shows my mother's parents with a phone at our address. I assume the new house on 54th Street wasn't ready when they moved out of their two-flat. My sister Barbara, who would have turned four that August, says she can't quite remember them staying over.

*I*t was during one of our visits that my father began talking about his job at Ford. I'm sure it happened in the usual way, with everyone at the kitchen table eating some kind of dessert; this was how we honored the bakers on both sides of the family. Most likely he would have started between pieces of coffee cake: "Every day you lined up outside the gates and waited for the foreman. He'd come out and point, 'You, you, and you. Everybody else, maybe tomorrow.'"

He related this as matter of fact, without bitterness or the explanation "That's why I joined the union," though he was a union man who made sure to get an Honorable Withdrawal Card from the UAW in 1944 before starting his job with the fire department. Most of all, my father was the son of immigrants, to whom such things happened. The 1930 Census lists him as "body polisher, Ford shop." His mother is both "head of household" and "clerk, bakery shop." One of her relatives owned it.

My mother had stories too, as when she and a girlfriend ventured far beyond the South Side to watch Hack Wilson play. This was years before any ivy clung to the walls at Wrigley Field. There were also tales of work. Once, during the depression, a man propositioned her. She turned down the chance—if it really existed—to make Argo cornstarch in exchange for a little sex.

She was employed at a paint factory the time a coworker caught something in his eye. Using a matchstick for a prop, she flipped back his eyelid to flush out a splinter. She learned the trick from her father. He was a small man I mostly remember from pictures and root-beer-flavored candy, in the shape of tiny barrels, that he carried in his sweater pocket. I am often told we bear a strong resemblance.

Chicago firefighters work twenty-four-hour shifts followed by two days off. The schedule allows for what my father called "hobby jobs," like driving a tanker truck filled with heating oil. The work gave him an unexpected sense of power: "I'd be up in the cab with all that fuel around me." Cars knew not to cut in front of him. But he hated making deliveries in the suburb of Riverside, where Frederick Law Olmsted decreed that no residential street should go uncurved. The same held true for intersections.

My father took great pride in his driving, without having so much as a creased fender into his eighties. Over the years he drove a variety of trucks, including fire engines; he even sat atop a hook-and-ladder as the tiller man. To him steering wheels were joysticks, however defined. And the level of performance he expected of himself on the street he demanded from his children.

My sisters Barbara and Betty Lou suffered the misfortune of learning to drive on a column shift with a teacher who did not tolerate the slightest grinding of gears. I was spared their fate when the Biscayne gave way to a Plymouth with push-button automatic. But there was no escaping my father's insistence that a good driver knew when and how to "buffalo," or get ahead, as traffic demanded. If our father told us to make a left-hand turn, *Now*, we obeyed without question. It did not help to show fear, and it was impossible to refuse him.

He would sacrifice the perfection of a new car to make his point. A few weeks before my driver's exam, we went out in our green 1970 Galaxie; when he could afford to buy off the showroom floor, my father was a loyal Ford man. We drove to an old defense plant where Ford once built engines for the air force. By the mid-1960s some of the buildings had been converted into a mall. Coincidence, or fate, determined the name of Ford City.

My father pointed out a parking space, but I backed in too hard. Do it again, he said, and again I misjudged. This went on a third and a fourth time, until I had scratched enough lines on the left rear fender for a polygraph test. How could he deny not wanting to beat me within an inch of my life? If nothing else, he turned all three children into masters of parallel parking.

Special license plates went on the Galaxie. A combination of six letters and numbers identified an automobile and the life of the man who owned it. EB 5415 truly was Edwin Bukowski, down to the street address that always mattered most to him. My father then arranged for me to have DB 5415 on my first car. It was an honor I let slip away for no good reason.

Driving—and Zane Grey novels—were my father's escape from the demands of work. We drove everywhere, provided he was not at the firehouse or Wesco Spring, the steadiest of his hobby jobs. From the back seat of the family car I grew familiar with the gargoyles in

Hyde Park long before I realized they were attached to buildings that comprised the University of Chicago.

It was the same with city parks. I assumed every family drove to one so their son could play on the swings or explore tropical plants that flourished under the great glass domes of the Garfield Park conservatory. We stopped going when the surrounding neighborhood changed from white to black.

Where other children grew sick or bored in the car, I counted myself lucky: Captain Cook had recruited me for his crew on the *Endeavour*. Among the early voyages I remember was one during the summer of 1960. We spent the better part of a week driving the city in search of the best deal on a new washer and dryer. To this day I half-think of eternity as my first encounter with Milwaukee Avenue, a busy street that cuts diagonally through the North Side of Chicago and beyond. God is the star appliance salesman at Polk Brothers.

Sundays we might drive to a vegetable stand outside the city or to the Baha'i Temple in Wilmette. We often stopped to eat at roadhouses, once remote places that had survived Prohibition; the back rooms where Bridgeport boys went drinking had been remodeled to serve us family fare. During our trips I thought it important to watch the gas gauge and report my findings every half hour or so. Even though patience was among his lesser virtues, my father never complained.

Five times when he grew sick I drove him to the hospital, and twice he went by ambulance. I could never be sure how close behind death followed. It began in 1998 when my sister brought everyone over for a Labor Day barbecue. The evening capped a summer that had seen his steady decline.

Every June my parents went to northern Wisconsin to fish, together with Barbara and her husband Bill. This was my sister's attempt at a fountain of youth where she could be a child again; I have a few pictures of our great family adventures into the deep woods and quiet lakes north of the Illinois border. With luck, over dinner her parents would address one another as Shorty and Mr. B, so it could be 1957 again. But this vacation the memories stayed away. My father barely walked, and his eldest child was deeply worried.

After hearing about the trip, I dropped by the house for a visit. My father spoke to me the way he always did, with a brevity that belied his intelligence. He had a good time, but the fish weren't biting. And your sister smokes too much. He was more concerned about that morning; he had come down with double vision and couldn't read the paper at breakfast. It was the funniest thing, he said. Two months later he did not make an effort to shave for his eighty-fifth birthday.

On Labor Day he mostly slept in a living room chair that he himself had bought a little before my birth in 1952. The one time he went to the bathroom he wet himself. At dinner he told Barbara and my mother to "Go to Hell and leave me alone" when they kept after him to finish his food; his weight had dropped to 146 pounds. Our daughter Clare, who was just starting first grade, never before saw her grandfather act this way; she tried her best not to cry. Afterward, when we helped him into the van, he thanked Michele "for everything." It was not clear if he meant that night or the past twenty years. We decided to put him in the hospital.

He was asleep when I came for him at noon the next day. During breakfast he had promised my mother to eat more; then he went back to bed. Eventually I was able to get him up and dressed. Seeing my father naked still made me uncomfortable. The wall of privacy between parent and adult child had yet to be fully breached.

Somehow we managed the front stairs to the car. On our way to Holy Cross, he wanted to know why construction work along 55th Street wasn't going faster; this would make for bad driving come winter. His voice sounded so weak I doubted he would ever see December. But he did, three more times.

I wish now that I had photographed my father's hands. They were the one part of his body that refused to succumb to age, even after arthritis had bent the fingertips at odd angles; seven decades of work left its residue in his grip. Once, two months after his eighty-third birthday, he drove over and helped me punch a hole in the wall to vent a dryer; previous owners of the house had run the exhaust through an open door in the basement. My father thrived on undoing the incompetence of others.

He made one concession to age that day by letting me help. At home he often complained that I was as useless to him as tits on a bull, or how I would screw up a one-car funeral. The second one he spoke as a racial slur. Such talk was common where we lived.

But that afternoon the work went easy. For two hours a small sledgehammer and chisel passed between us. We ended up covered in dust, which bothered him no more than mud does a ten-year-old. He fit the vent into its hole before cementing the gaps shut. Another job well done by Eddie Bukowski, he always said.

The photographer Lewis Hine would have been drawn to my father, either as victim or hero. During the Progressive Era, Hine documented such unpleasant realities as urban poverty and child labor. His picture of "Polish Boy Taking Noon Rest in Doffer Box/Quidnick Mill/1909" shows a child of eleven or twelve leaning against the kind of textile machine that often mangled young limbs and lives. It is an extraordinary photo, though not one that enraged the public to the point of demanding change. So my father was left to experience the injustice of child labor for himself.

By the 1920s Hine had grown weary of documenting social conditions. He looked again at the world of work, this time for inspiration more positive. "Cities do not build themselves," he wrote, "machines cannot make machines unless back of them all are the brains and toil of men." It was a belief that led Hine to record the efforts of those men whose toil made possible the Empire State Building.

His subjects catch rivets above the streets of Manhattan with a New York nonchalance, as Willie Mays did later at the Polo Grounds. One man dangles from a cable a thousand feet in the air while others are content merely to perch on the edge of eternity. The occasional smile does not intrude on an overwhelming sense of purpose. If anyone betrayed the slightest sign of fear or doubt, Hine must have turned his lens elsewhere.

My father never doubted. As long as his body allowed, Edwin Bukowski found work by grabbing a cable on its way up to the top floor. Only he came home smelling of smoke from warehouse fires that burned all night while his family lay asleep in bed. And he used nails for rivets. They worked just as well to reassemble an almost-new garage he saved from demolition, or fasten the shingles he and his friends laid for a new roof on the house.

The fire department made him retire after a career of thirty-four years. It should have been thirty-three, but no one caught the lie on his birth certificate. Because he could not rest, my father went to work for a plating supply company.

There were deliveries to make under the El tracks on Lake Street and out by O'Hare, where the cornfields had given way to industrial parks. At day's end he returned home content in his exhaustion. Hauling chemicals was a last chance for him to work oh so high, a breeze in his face, the steel beams a ladder pointed to the sun. Then he got old.

So did my mother, though in ways different. All through that first summer of his decline she insisted on following her routine: Fridays to the hairdresser and the third Monday of the month to the seniors' club in the church basement. It was a surprise each time she returned home to find her husband fighting to get up off the living room floor.

My mother loved fashion. I do not mean that she was disagreeably shallow or vain. Rather, clothes were a tool in the struggle for self-expression. They also caused the one great act of defiance in her life. Nothing my father could say or threaten kept his wife from taking a job at Ford City, where she sold women's clothes. The hospital smocks failed to do her justice.

After we buried one parent, I tried to make a deal, that the other would remain healthy provided she kept active. But there were no takers, and my mother began to slip away. As part of my end in this failed bargain, I took her to Brookfield Zoo, a place we often visited on family trips. It was a perfect Saturday in early June, warm and not yet humid, with spray from the Roosevelt Fountain touching our foreheads. A circle of bronze animal skulls borders the reflecting pool. Each one used to be gilded in the manner of my father's work.

The zoo is filled with rock formations. Some are real, others are cement forms that make up the outdoor exhibits. My mother had seen these shapes perhaps a hundred times in her life. But that afternoon they made her think she was in a cemetery. I blamed it on the too-many pills she ingested each day. They proved the need for those disclaimers about possible side effects.

A series of infections took her out of the house in August. It began with cellulitis in the right leg. After two weeks she was transferred from Holy Cross to a rehabilitation center. There she contracted Clostridium difficile, a stomach infection; urinary tract and eye problems tagged along with the C-dif. She stayed five weeks before returning to the hospital, where a blood clot developed in the infected leg. My mother had gone, in the center's terminology, from moderate to maximum assist. At the age of eighty-eight she was made to endure illness without the comfort of attending to matters of appearance. Only then did the roots of her hair finally begin to show grey.

My mother now freely mixed together memories, either as a symptom of senility or as a defense against sleeping in so many strange beds. I grew used to being Michael, or I listened to her sing: "You're the one for me, Honey / No one else will do, Honey." She said the words were from my father's favorite song.

Sometimes we experienced her life this way, and sometimes I told the stories from old. She lay in bed listening to me talk about her mother's devotion to cod liver oil or the adult-ed typing classes she took when I was a boy; because the secretaries working downtown were by her definition sophisticated, my mother tried to learn the keyboard and smoke cigarettes the way her sister Lou did. It was a very good day for me if she recalled selling clothes at Ford City.

In the wake of death and dementia, I am left with pictures of home. They have become too valuable to let sit on a closet shelf.

Stanley with Chester, Elizabeth,
and the baby Ed

Ed and Mary Ann,
June 17, 1939

Camp MacDonald, 1926

II

BRIDGEPORT

I have this memory, a picture really, from the age of four. My father is sitting alongside me on a Western Avenue streetcar that will let us off at Riverview Amusement Park. Our intention is, just as Two-Ton Baker urged on television, to laugh our troubles away. Other than a serious case of asthma, I cannot honestly say what my worries might have been in the year 1956.

There is another time maybe two or three years later, again with my father. It is a warm Sunday afternoon following church. The branches of the elm trees along Homan Avenue sway in a September breeze that, for fun, has knocked some baseball cards out of my hand. I manage to round them up before they can blow into the street, where good boys dare not go, if only for fear of getting caught.

Soon enough my father walks down the front steps to the car, and it's time for our weekend drive. We are going to visit his mother in Bridgeport, with its magnificent churches and corner taverns. On our way we pass the Union Stock Yards. The cattle pens still seem without end.

American cities all have neighborhoods that define them, the way Bridgeport does Chicago. It would be safe to say my father grew up in another Brooklyn, only different. Bridgeporters are not the type to reminisce about the good old days. Nostalgia rarely settles on a place once known as Hardscrabble.

The area was settled by an impoverished people who had fled starvation for the prospect of backbreaking labor. A popular saying of the time was that the three ingredients needed for building a canal were a pick, a shovel, and an Irishman. Contractors on the Illinois and Michigan Canal took an interest in tools only. The Irish repaid that favor in a variety of ways, not the least of which occurred during groundbreaking ceremonies in Bridgeport on the Fourth of July, 1836: visiting dignitaries were met with a shower of stones. It was still raining the day a Polish immigrant gave birth to her second surviving child, Edwin Joseph, on August 18, 1913.

My father never bought into the notion of belonging to the greatest generation in American history. He had spent too much of his life identified with one social problem or another. "The majority of gangs in Chicago are of Polish stock," wrote the sociologist Frederic Thrasher in his acclaimed study of *The Gang*, "[and] this may be due to the fact that there are in the city more than 150,000 more persons of Polish extraction than of any other nationality except the German." Bridgeport comprised that part of Chicago Thrasher called "The South Side Badlands." This would explain my father's love of Westerns.

In the 1920s gangs—as distinct from gangsters—did not shoot at one another; they fought with fists and baseball bats. They did not sell or use drugs, though the home brew of Prohibition is another story. And they did not use cans of spray paint. Instead teenage boys looked for ways to win a Kewpie doll, which they broke into pieces for the chalk to write their graffiti. They did steal and they did miss school and they did have sex, at the risk of marrying the girl if she became pregnant.

Then, as if on cue or by instinct, most of them got over it. My father did not comment much on his gang days beyond saying, "We beat on the Turkeys good," or "You knew not to walk on that block alone." In some ways Bridgeport differed little from the Balkans.

I was no stranger to the school where Thrasher earned his doctorate. We often drove by the University of Chicago on the way to see my uncle after he moved his dental practice to Commercial Avenue, near the steel mills. Thrasher studied under the great Robert Park, who made a career of observing the behavior of primitive peoples; they inhabited vast stretches of the city beyond his office window. "It is the slum, the city wilderness, as it has been called, which provides the city gang with its natural habitat," Park wrote in his 1927 preface to Thrasher. The good news, presumably, was that gangs could be studied and "they can be controlled."

By his own admission, my father was part of a Bridgeport gang. He did not hang alone. Thrasher belonged to the Chicago School of sociology, which is to say he did not write alone. Subject and student both used language to signal their affiliations. It was a Young Disciple who commented on "the extensive demoralization which exists in the Polish-American community." Where University of Chicago sociologists William I. Thomas and Florian Znaniecki led, Thrasher willingly followed.

In 1918 Thomas and Znaniecki published *The Polish Peasant in Europe and America*, a collection of some eight hundred letters written in the first years of the twentieth century. To recount a modern-day Exodus would seem to be humbling work, if only humility mattered to street gangs or social scientists. Thomas and Znaniecki said they wanted to show "the difference between unreflective social cohesion brought about by tradition, and reflective social co-operation brought about by rational selection of common ends and means." These were, in their own way, fighting words, as observers called out the observed.

Brawls are a great if misunderstood Chicago tradition. The city did not suddenly turn into Beirut by the Lake, as the *Wall Street Journal* wrote in the 1980s, because a black mayor and a white city council haggled over the spoils of politics. Chicago as fight card dates to at least the War of 1812, when soldiers and Indians butchered one another in the sand dunes south of Fort Dearborn.

The problem with violence is the way it can threaten civic pretense. Eventually Chicagoans worked out an understanding whereby the worst bloodletting was confined, more or less, to the Union Stock Yards. This bit of compassion freed the city to cultivate the sport of boxing, with a stable of fighters representing person and place. The contest between Hyde Park and Bridgeport went the full fifteen rounds, stretching out over my father's lifetime into mine.

Most academics deny this side of professional life. They would rather see themselves as scholars or scholar activists. Truth is the prize, as an end in itself or as the means to foster social change. But the boxing trunks are a dead giveaway, along with the excuse of wearing them for a friend.

My father knew how to give a punch to his words. When we drove along the Midway Plaisance, he would point to the university buildings and say, "See this place? You go in Catholic and come out Communist." A smart boxer baited an opponent with insults that cut; truth was immaterial. Muhammad Ali was one of many South Siders to appreciate this. Ed Bukowski was another.

The beauty of boxing lies in its sounds and rhythms: the ringside bell, padded glove to flesh, a flurry of punches and counterpunches. It is a spectacle intoxicating to watch. But few fighters walk away untouched. I can only hope that my father gave as good as he got.

He hurt from being told for so long that members of the working class were, alas, prone to dysfunction. He was the boy without a father, an education, or a white-collar skill. It did not matter that he made himself into a decent parent or buffaloed his way into the middle class by dint of an axe and hose. Once injured, he never fully healed. Of course, he no more acknowledged this pain than he would tip his punches.

It was on our drives that my father could be made to feel the sting of privilege. Suburbs along the North Shore did not exactly welcome all light-skinned people equally; family memories of Ellis Island had a way of leading to the service entrance only. Whatever their beauty, all those trees and mansions covered Sheridan Road with the soft deception of a velvet glove. We should have avoided these towns, but my father had a weakness for pretty places.

I ignored evidence of injury throughout my college years. Our arguments kept me from noticing. We disagreed over everything from national politics to how much milk was left in the pitcher after cereal. If my mother happened into the room, he would tell me, "You're talking like a sausage." Other times I sounded like a "busted asshole." Richard Nixon brought out the worst in people.

My father cared little for Nixon, a president he deemed inferior to "the pegleg," Franklin Roosevelt. But the ex-fighter imagined Thrasher everywhere. That was how he understood Watergate reporters and, on occasion, his son. It could have gotten bad between us if not for a mutual lifeline. We each read the box scores and agreed that the White Sox mostly stunk.

I wonder how many of his friends were this way, punch-drunk from self-inflicted doubt. My father was extraordinarily gifted with his hands; every project he undertook seemed to spur his curiosity in the physical world around him. He tinkered, took apart, and reassembled. He was the only person I knew to keep two electric motors by his workbench, one with a grinding wheel to sharpen his tools and the other for backup. But this gift did not count for much outside the basement or garage. So it was for the other men on the block, their dreams bound by the extension cord running out to a circular saw.

When I was a boy of twelve, my mother had me do something she would not, to fetch her husband from the tavern on 55th Street. This was Tee Zee's, a true hole-in-the-wall or, as my father put it, a typical gin mill. I shadowed him, mostly on weekends in good weather, for two years. It was around the time my father turned fifty.

Sometimes he smiled at the sight of me and shrugged his shoulders, like a child caught in the act. That meant he was in a good mood. I could expect a penny pretzel rod from the container on the bar or a quart bottle of Canfield's orange soda. Otherwise it was "Tell her I'll be there in a while." Either way, I could see that he did not drink alone.

This was, I think, his mid-life crisis. Because he never took the officers' exam for the fire department, other men gave the commands that ordered his day. The arthritis in his back sought a more direct control over him, with pain that diminished the ability he had to work without regard to time or comfort. He was also a father with girls who were leaving home for college and a son who remained a mystery to him. So he sat on a bar stool, his hands cupped around a bottle of Old Style, wanting perspective only to have a boy come call him home to Sunday dinner. It was hard for me to open the screen door that led inside Tee Zee's; I was both a minor and a trespasser. More than once I told my mother he wasn't there.

For the longest time I saw my father as this force of nature in human form, always to be observed, at a safe distance if possible. His schedule cooperated during most of my adolescence. Periodically the fire house and Wesco lined up so that he worked thirteen consecutive days.

Saturday was his half-day, ending around one o'clock. For lunch he might want a can of soup or a fried baloney sandwich; the pan was left for me to scrub. Then he would start to work around the house. There was always wash to do and weeds to pull in the vegetable garden. He and my mother canned tomatoes every fall. Sunday would be the firehouse.

As a boy, I understood neither his devotion to work nor its origins. All I saw was routine, like the seasons following one upon the other. It was winter, my father put snow tires on the car. It was spring, he started painting. It was summer, he laid a new floor in the kitchen. It was fall, he covered the rose bushes. But we never played catch the way other fathers and sons did.

*S*o began my search for heroes. Looking back, I realize the choice of Hyde Park was no accident. My life has been filled with small acts of rebellion, a few of them meaningful. This one started so easily: my parents didn't know to be impressed by dead people with university degrees. John Dewey, Thorstein Veblen, and Harold Ickes all seemed unique in ways I could only hope to be.

My favorite was Ickes, an acerbic lawyer and political activist. I also liked Veblen's idea that the wealthy were given to displays of conspicuous consumption. Dogs, though, always struck me as a poor example; for a boy with asthma, they were more of a dream deferred. Dewey I never fully understood, perhaps because seventeen years of Catholic education left a mark.

Ickes managed the 1911 mayoral campaign of Charles Merriam, the University of Chicago political scientist turned politician who fell a mere seventeen thousand votes short of victory. In some Chicago circles, until Harold Washington there was no greater achievement than to make the city almost ready for reform. That explains my fool's errand during the mayoral primary of 1975—I rang doorbells in my precinct for Bill Singer, the last liberal opponent of Richard J. Daley.

Ickes also headed the local chapter of the NAACP in the 1920s before serving as FDR's sole secretary of the interior and most aggressive defender. His description of 1940 Republican presidential candidate Wendell Willkie as that "simple, bare-foot Wall Street lawyer" still makes me smile. The Bush family is fortunate this critic of privilege died the year of my birth.

Ickes's autobiography turned me into an acolyte of the truest sort. I adopted his friends and enemies as my own, though hardly any of them were living. And I smiled at being called a curmudgeon, the nickname Ickes took for himself. I even worked him into my senior thesis. My problem stemmed from not knowing when to quit.

Anyone earning a college degree in 1974 felt the touch of Watergate. So it was for me. I chose law over journalism because of an inability to experience disappointment in more than one profession at a time. My thought was to copy the reform career of Ickes by enrolling in law school. I chose the one that graduated Daleys senior and junior. Ickes's alma mater, the University of Chicago, cost too much.

Outside of a class in constitutional law, De Paul University left me ill-prepared for the world of torts and moot court. My professors had mostly wanted to be friends with their students, so we arranged our desks in circles and called one another by our first names. Two months after graduation I found that the tables in law school classrooms were bolted to the floor. The chairs moved only with great effort.

Had someone told me to attend lectures in the nude, I would have done so without question. That was how little I knew of the professional world beyond Homan Avenue. My single, shining moment testified to what a poor fit the law and I made. One day in contracts, I briefed a case on liability for some object—a tug boat or oil rig, I can no longer recall which—lost at sea.

Hands shot up the instant I finished, which was never a good sign. My classmates felt compelled to point out, with extreme prejudice if possible, an egregiously wrong answer. Only they had fallen for a trap in the facts that I never even saw; worse yet, their view of the case made more sense to me than my own correct answer did. After class I wondered how often an attorney could depend on this level of serendipity, or dumb luck. I dropped out a few weeks later.

Rather than tell anyone, I pretended to attend class for another month. Most days I explored the city the way my father had done with us on weekends. There were boulevards to drive and feats of architecture to behold, like Sears' old headquarters on the West Side. This complex of buildings filled forty acres, including a colonnaded garden that sat by the main entrance. I remembered going there once with my parents; down the street a vendor sold Italian ice from his pushcart. I thrilled at seeing something that took 23 million bricks to build, though corporate flight has now reduced that number.

During my few weeks of law school I read Chicago novels in order to ward off the onset of a legalistic mentality. Afterward I half expected the characters of Algren and Farrell to materialize either out of appreciation or curiosity. Frankie Machine and Studs Lonigan were not so inclined. George Pullman was another disappointment. I drove out to his company town with its quaint row houses and legacy of failed paternalism. Mr. Pullman could not be enticed to leave his grave at Graceland, where he lay under a protective blanket of concrete and railroad ties. Perhaps he doubted my intentions.

Still, the city made enough of an impression for me to pursue the study of urban history. I even planned to make Ickes the star of my dissertation. But in the quiet of a climate-controlled reading room at the Library of Congress, I found myself to be as poor a judge of historical character as I had been of legal fact. Both at home and at work, Ickes demonstrated a real knack for playing the bad guy.

He abandoned Chicago to use his wife's money and build a mansion in a secluded section of the North Shore. "The bathtub in our room drains slowly," he complained in a letter to his architect, "indicating some obstruction, and I would like to have all drains tested."

Ickes also found fault with his window shades ("I do not see the necessity of two cords"), storage space ("I don't see how some of our shelving could have been more badly planned"), and floors ("I will not accept squeaky floors in any part of the house"). He twice hung up on his architect "because it seemed to me that further discussion over the telephone was worse than profitless to both of us."

Nowhere in his papers did I find my imagined hero. If anything, Ickes the New Dealer proved as petty as Ickes the homeowner. He divided people into enemies, those who opposed the president, and rivals, anyone who might visit the Oval Office ahead of him. It was hard to tell the difference.

In 1933 Ickes answered a letter from his former law partner Donald Richberg, who worried that Ickes's selection to the cabinet had hurt his own chances for a position. The new secretary of the interior responded as anything but the gracious victor: "You cleverly adopt the feminine device of conducting a whining offensive under the pretense of defending yourself against a purely imaginary injury." Yet this was the same official who arranged with Eleanor Roosevelt to have Marian Anderson sing on the steps of the Lincoln Memorial on Easter Sunday 1939. If there was a way to reconcile these extremes in personality, it remained hidden among the 150,000 items that Ickes left in his collection.

I entered graduate school wanting a Ph.D. as a sign of learning, only to leave with a degree that brought me back to my father. He checked his own drains, and, in contrast to Ickes, remained faithful to his wife. He also let me have a dog when I reached the sixth grade.

A little over a year before my father's death, I did a magazine piece on Ickes's Tudor estate by the lake; the current owners allowed me in for a look. Another journalist could have imagined the visit by Teddy Roosevelt to the house in 1916, of how a proud man never impressed by the ostentation of others was reduced to making small talk with well-wishers gathered in the sun room. But what impressed me most of all was the woodwork in the servants' quarters. It consisted simply of varnished boards with a curve on top, the same as in our house. Life, I realized, is about knowing one's place.

*T*his is not to say that Ickes and other members of his Hyde Park gang were without merit or honor, just that they were held to looser standards than their counterparts in Bridgeport. But it does no good to hold a grudge. Thomas and Znaniecki, I admit, did put a human face on the phenomenon of immigration by finding letters such as the one about the girl "going to America, also to Chicago." She "boasted that she is going to a sweetheart. She told it only to me, but people are also talking about it. Amen."

Such dreams often led to the reality of Morgan Street, as did the advice that, "if you have money, it would be perhaps better for you to buy a house in Chicago than a farm. Now, don't be angry with me for giving you advice, but I, as your mother, want you to live the best possible [way]. Now, you see, there are many people from our country, but they all settle in Chicago."

Immigration exists as one of the most unsettling constants in American life. The arrival of my grandparents' generation drove Congress to restriction and sociologists to further research. With the gates safely shut after passage of the National Origins Act of 1924, Thrasher set about not to condemn but to study. "We are merely describing the soil which favors the growth of gangs," he wrote. "Such underlying conditions as inadequate family life, poverty, deteriorating neighborhoods, and ineffective religion, education and recreation must be considered together as a situation complex which forms the matrix of gang development."

The subjects of Thrasher's research all look to be of a type, or sound that way. Boys shout, "Jigs, de bulls!" at the approach of a policeman, and they chant, "De furder y'go, de tougher it gets—/I live at Toity-Toid and de tracks,/De last house on de corner,/An dere's blood on de door." But the echo is not Chicago.

Ordinarily South Siders stand out for the way we drop our g's and play with d's. We may say, "I'm goin' to a Hunert and Secon' Street," but rarely do we give an East Coast inflection to "Turty-turd." Yet Thrasher heard boys speak in a mix of Barney Google and the Bowery. An ungenerous critic might go so far as to charge him with preconceptions, if not prejudices.

His focus on gangs led Thrasher away from such a person as my grandmother, which is a shame, since Elizabeth Skonieczny Bukowski stood out as a strikingly attractive woman nearly six feet tall in heels. She had about her a look of perpetual self-assurance framed by wire-rimmed glasses. In her wedding picture she sits so as not to tower over her husband. That would be my Grandfather Stanley, though he never lived to be called that. He died when his son Edwin was not yet thirteen months old.

In the years since I joined the profession, history has become a home to mediums who trade in probate records and Census reports. Little else is needed to create communities where the dead speak with strikingly postmodern voices. My powers in this regard are sorely lacking. I can recall most of my Bridgeport relatives only as a collection of blurred faces and names. *Ciocia* Jenny and *Wujek* Jim were, no doubt, as good to me as any (great) aunt and uncle could be, but I cannot make them speak on the subject of my grandfather. He sits there, silent, next to his wife in the two photographs of him that survive.

But I learned enough tricks to flesh out a few details of his life. On the South Side of Chicago, most Poles await the Second Coming while at rest in Resurrection Cemetery; it is located in a suburb just a few blocks from the factory complex that may or may not have held a job for my mother in the 1930s. Depending on wind direction, the smell of cornstarch comes as part of a visit to the grave of a loved one.

Cemetery records show that Stanley died September 9, 1914. The burial arrangements were common for the time. My grandfather's body was put into a "term grave," with a kind of meter attached. Because she was poor, my grandmother in effect rented the plot. After thirty years the body was disinterred and placed in a common grave, exactly where the cemetery can't say. Here was another of my father's secrets. Other arrangements could have been made at term's end in 1944, since he and his mother had more money to spend. But no one did.

When his microfilm machines are in the mood, the Cook County clerk also provides certain types of information. The clerk will, for seven dollars, copy and mail out a death certificate. This piece of paper often details a life as fully as its passing. So it is with Stanislaw Bukowski, born in 1883 to Joseph and a mother listed as Unknown.

Stanley immigrated to America in 1905 and spent the remainder of his life in Chicago. For eight of those nine years he worked as a "cement sidewalk layer." Death found him in an apartment at 3112 Wall Street; there is no way of knowing if he saw the irony attached to such a street name. The physician of record, Dr. Mariski on Archer Avenue, certified that he treated Stanley for one day, July 20, seven weeks before his death. Unfortunately the doctor recorded the cause of death in a barely decipherable scrawl. As best anyone can tell, Stanley succumbed to a combination of rheumatism and heart disease.

Yet other of our family secrets were stored in a safe deposit box at Talman Savings and Loan, on the corner of 55th Street and Kedzie Avenue. My mother and I often walked the four blocks there from our house to the basement vault. A clerk retrieved the box for us to take into a cubicle, roughly the same size as my closet hideout. We sat in total darkness save for the light from a small table lamp that fell on whatever document my mother held in her hands. There were always deeds and policies to attend to.

These trips together ended around 1960. In the time since, a Dutch banking conglomerate has taken over Talman, and the remodeled viewing rooms allow in too much light; the shadows from *Citizen Kane* are all gone. But a box can still be had for the right key, which I used to find a copy of my father's birth certificate.

He was born at home, 3229 South Morgan. It is a corner building typical of old Chicago, done in brown brick, with a store on the first floor and apartments above. The most striking features are the second-story turret and the flagpole rising from its roof. A flag may well have flown over the apartment that third Monday in August to signal the arrival of yet another child with Star-Spangled eyes. In working-class Chicago, that was indeed a fortunate son.

These home births were once common. There was another just eight blocks away in a two-flat at 35th and Lowe, where Richard J. Daley was born in 1902. The future mayor and the future firefighter who served him shared an unquestioning love of country, if little else. The Daleys always lived in a different part of Bridgeport, where the son of a sheet-metal worker could avoid the assembly line for something better. It helped to have two parents.

Question 20 (a) of my father's birth certificate asks, "Number of children born to this mother and including this birth[?]" The answer provided is four. Question 20 (b) follows with, "Number of children living at time of this birth[?]" The answer is one. That would be Chester, my Uncle Doc. The births and, presumably, infant deaths of two other siblings were never mentioned in conversation.

Three weeks before his death, I asked my father when his mother had come to the United States, but he didn't know. The past in its own right did not interest him the way it did me. When she died, the paper trail that marked Elizabeth's life from Poland to Bridgeport probably was discarded as clutter. Instead my father chose to keep boxes of incense; each piece looked like candy corn shaded a dark grey. He lit some pieces in the basement a few times after the funeral. They emitted a smell that, though sweet, could not entice the dead to appear.

I had better luck with those documents that constitute the public record. Three times my Grandma Bukowski declared her intention to become a citizen. The first was December 7, 1914, when the twenty-nine-year-old widow "Bukowska" went to Superior Court. She tried again in Circuit Court ten years later as Elizabeth Ponicki. Her petition was granted, finally, in the U.S. District Court of Chicago, January 1948. The form includes a snapshot with the signature Elizabeth Bukowska.

There must have been a legal requirement for her to sign the oath of allegiance as Elizabeth Ponicki. Twenty years earlier she had gone to court to free herself of that name. *Ponicki v. Ponicki* was filed July 8, 1927. In the trial transcript my grandmother testified to being married four months, from May to September 1917, before her husband abandoned her. How did you treat him during the time you were married to him? "I treated him good." And he left you and family? "Yes, sir."

Her husband's lawyer responded that his client "was compelled to go out by harsh and vilifying language, often repeated, and that he went out to avoid threatened violence and disorder," and that was why he stayed away. Perhaps because the lawyer left out the part about Anton Ponicki leaving a woman four months pregnant, the judge ruled against him. My grandmother won the right, as she requested, to "resume the name of Elizabeth Bukowski, the name by a former husband." She also asked for "such further and other relief . . . according to equity and good conscience," but there is no indication in the file or the life she led that this included the slightest financial support.

My father had little use for the kind of sentiment that led me to find information on Elizabeth; the course of his life did not encourage it. There was one exception, in 1977, after an invitation arrived in the mail for a cousins' picnic. Why bother, I thought, since he kept in touch with all three of his cousins? Only my count was off by twenty-five or more. Elizabeth had been one of eight brothers and sisters.

I learned as much on the first Sunday of August when we drove out to a Polish National Alliance campground fifty miles southwest of Chicago. There, among the cornfields, the children of Bridgeport returned to one another. I keep a snapshot of that first reunion under the glass on my dresser.

One after another person asked me that day, "You're Ed's boy, aren't you?" which I was. But who were they and where had they been all this time? My father's response of "That's your cousin" did little to end the confusion. For the first few years I was as a child lost in a wilderness of names—and faces that bore more than a passing resemblance to mine. In the eighth year of the picnic, one of the cousins produced a family tree and history, so I had a document to work from. That would have been the time to begin oral histories, to see if anyone had actually encountered the likes of Frederic Thrasher, but I was as yet too shy for anything so bold. Mostly I collected fragments of stories to piece together at some later time.

The cousins as children had been very close. Then something happened—a move out of the neighborhood, perhaps school or marriage. In the case of my grandmother's sister Helen, it was a return to Poland with her husband and family. Stanley Barczak apparently ordered the *Wehrmacht* off his farm one day in September 1939; Poles have an irrational attachment to their land. The Germans responded with a finality they soon made commonplace.

Stanley's children managed to survive the war and return to the United States. I remember the son in particular. He was said to have been so handsome a boy that the authorities in Poland mistook him for Aryan; they compounded their error by inviting him to join the Hitler Youth. Again I was too shy to ask. Each summer we shook hands, after which he bowed, a shock of white hair tumbling over his forehead. He was a hemophiliac who fell victim to HIV contracted from a blood transfusion.

The family tree and history were the work of Alice, the sister of one of the three cousins I knew. Until the picnics, I thought her brother was an only child. Alice proved to be a blessing, for reasons other than genealogy. She never failed to compliment me if she saw a letter or op-ed of mine in the newspaper, and she had an endless supply of *chrusciki*, bow-tie-shaped pastry that she carried with her from table to table. She left behind a most agreeable trail of crumbs and powdered sugar.

Alice listed Waclaw Kropidlowski as my grandmother's brother-in-law, which also made him my great-uncle. For more than fifteen years this information barely registered, since I had no recollection of the man. Then, after my father's death, I found Waclaw's name listed as the second-ever owner of my parents' house, purchased in June 1927. This was the "big bang" that began my universe a quarter of a century later.

My grandmother took formal possession of the house in 1933; my guess is she was renting it before that. For some reason Waclaw bought the house back on March 15, 1941, only to sell it to my father the same day. I imagine these transactions were all done out of family obligation. What kind of Kropidlowski turned his back on a Skonieczny or Bukowski?

The Home Owners' Loan Corporation, courtesy of Franklin Roosevelt, saved my grandmother from defaulting on the mortgage. "This indenture, made this first day of June A.D. 1934, between Elizabeth Bukowski, divorced and not remarried, and Edwin J. Bukowski, a bachelor, as joint tenants" was in the sum of $4,320, to be paid out in monthly installments of $34.16. Thus did the patrician president make possible the two-bedroom bungalow—with expandable attic— a world away from Bridgeport. As working-class people have said many times and in many ways, God bless the New Deal. On that Harold Ickes and I can agree.

Though helpful, Alice's research did not answer all my questions. Some information, like my grandmother's second marriage and the two children she lost, was missing. Alice either chose to skip over the more unpleasant details, or she never found the right source. I cannot ask which it was because, like so many other cousins, she has passed on.

Although we had twenty-four picnics, the adult children were not much interested in continuing the tradition. The truth is, the ties that bound our parents extended to only a few of us. They grew up "Skonieczny" and had older relatives who knew to distinguish between the feminine "Bukowska" and the masculine "Bukowski." Now we go by "Skoney" or "Skony" and use "Bukowski" only. Names were simplified, the number of relationships streamlined.

The poor and the newly arrived still value extended family, along with the Kennedys. But anyone then wanting to trade Bridgeport for the middle class was well advised to leave behind their peasant notions of kinship. The nuclear family, give or take the occasional relation, promised social mobility. So the cousins were given a choice between old ways and new.

First, however, they attempted a compromise. At the same time my father bought the house from Waclaw, his brother Doc took an apartment on the other side of the block; Harry, the other brother, bought a bungalow a half-block away. Some of the cousins also moved into the neighborhood. This failed replanting of Bridgeport still bothers me. I am always partial to stories of families rooted to a place over generations. My sense of community is admittedly simple.

But Homan Avenue was not the old country. For all the Polish spoken on the street, mine was a distinctly American, albeit Catholic,
neighborhood. Here too people harbored postwar dreams of leaving
their bungalow for a ranch or split-level in the suburbs. If they resis-
ted at first, the real estate section could afford to wait. There was always the chance that an ad next week would do the trick, or one of the
sitcoms set in Sunnydale; everything looked so new. When racial un-
rest convulsed the South Side in the 1960s, dreams stampeded into
fact. The brothers moved, one before my birth even and the other after I reached high school. In the end only my father stayed.

Sometimes on a weekend we took the car to new developments
outside Chicago. The idea of suburban living was so foreign to me I
never learned the names of the places we visited. Unlike other parts of
my life, these memories float unconnected to any city place.

My parents were responding to the great urge of the day—they
had to see what the fuss was about. We walked into houses so new that
the contractors hadn't bothered to sand the floors yet or even sweep up
the lumps of plaster. Asthma gave me a definite sense of what "new"
smelled like. It was an acute mix of fresh paint and sawdust that could
trigger an attack if I stayed inside too long.

My parents said little, and nothing I could overhear, as we moved
from one room to another. Maybe the house was too small, or Mayor
Daley announced he would crack down on the residency requirement
for city workers. It is just as likely my parents never intended to do
anything more than look. They had avoided one life-changing
move—to Arizona, for my health—and did not want another. We beheld Levittown without entering.

Frederic Thrasher would have been surprised that any of his old
subjects even knew how to make the effort. In his call to "Give Life
Meaning for the Boy," Thrasher offered himself as an example. Unre-
formed gang members simply did not measure up: "I get my French

lesson even though I am tired and the night is hot and the task is tedious, whereas if I followed the impulse of the moment, I would take a swim in the lake or make an excursion with a friend to a soda fountain.

"I am enabled to control my behavior in this way because I wish to learn French in order to achieve the more ultimate purpose of taking a Ph.D. degree, reading the scientific works prepared by scholarly Frenchmen, and getting along comfortably during the year I am to live in Paris." Why can't the poor, he might well have asked, be more like me?

They were. My father and his cousins learned the same discipline that fueled the ambitious doctoral candidate, only it derived from other sources, like *A First Book in English for Non-English Speaking Adults*. This was a 1920s primer for adult-education classes conducted in city factories. Students from the assembly line were taught a language and a message, as in Lesson 32, Hours of Work:

> I get up at six o'clock.
> I eat my breakfast at seven o'clock.
> When I have finished my breakfast I walk to the shop.
> I go through the gate.
> I go into the shop and to my place.
> When the whistle blows we begin our work.
> When the whistle blows at noon we stop our work for lunch.
> At half past twelve we begin our work again.
> Every Saturday we stop work at noon.

There was more. Lesson 5, about a shoe store, advised, "Good shoes make work easy." The parts of the body were another subject for instruction. "We must keep our fingers out of the machine" just as "Goggles keep iron, steel and dust from the eyes." Students also learned that Time ("The time-keeper docked me for lost time / I had less pay because I lost time") was money: "I work ten hours a day, and I am paid 41 cents an hour."

The primer included several readings on civics. "The schools belong to all the people," noted Lesson 50, and "A child must go to school until he is 16, unless he has an employment certificate." The next five sentences detailed how to get one. Then, "If the child is well, and not too thin, they will give him a work certificate." Five lessons were devoted to good nutrition.

The Association of Commerce must have found a way to dissolve the *First Book* in the drinking water because, somehow, my father absorbed everything. He lived in a universe where life's opportunities followed a schedule that waited for no one. To be merely on time risked being late, which to him was one of the deadly sins comprising failure.

My sisters and I lived in a household for the hyperpunctual. The clock dictated when we would walk out the door for school and back in again; supper knew to appear on the table weekdays at 5:45 P.M., sharp. The spirit of Frederick Winslow Taylor haunted our family outings.

Because he was always the first one ready, my father would sit on the couch in the living room. Waiting was a form of torture for him. He mumbled, checked his watch, then mumbled a little louder. This continued until he could bear it no longer, at which point he yelled, "C'mon! Let's get a move on, will you?" Being just one shoe or earring shy of ready did not constitute a suitable defense. Somewhere a stopwatch was ticking.

Although the children of Bridgeport all learned the importance of time, the outside world withheld applause. It was not enough to take a primer's lessons to heart. Once branded, these subjects of scholarly research faced a lifetime of critical observation, as hard hats or Archie

Bunkers or Reagan Democrats. At best they were urban villagers whose love of a particular neighborhood could not withstand the cosmopolitan forces of modern life. The people in question simply did not qualify as "progressive" in any of the ways that mattered.

The picnics provided a communal defense, if for just one afternoon a year. They also allowed my father a more personal satisfaction; he had never been expected to make all that much of himself. While no one ever said so, it showed in the tone of surprise behind the comment of "You're Ed's boy." Since my father should have died young, I was not supposed to exist.

When my father was seven, a fire swept through the family's apartment. He always claimed to have told the fireman who found him in bed, "Leave me alone. I want to go to sleep." Either the child exhibited a stubborn streak or latent death wish.

He definitely liked to take risks. So he climbed a fence to watch Negro Leaguers play at South Side Park, and he swam in the polluted waters of the abandoned Illinois and Michigan Canal. Another favorite swimming spot were the quarries that lay just outside the city. Deep water did not frighten him, there or on Lake Erie in a rowboat that nearly capsized during a squall. (It happened during one of his trips east.) And of all the jobs Chicago had to offer, he chose to fight fires. None of his relatives did anything as dangerous. My father was a man who had to be taught to care about consequences.

One year at our picnic the cousins set up a bulletin board to display old family pictures. We brought one of my father alongside his brother Chester. They are sitting astride what are best described as four-wheeled, metal-framed horses with small handlebars for reins. My father is no more than five, his brother seven.

The difference in age and temperament is obvious. My uncle looks so much more confident, sure to succeed in that way the neighboring Irish had started to. My father is on the left, the shy one who then and always deferred to his brother. Only it was my uncle whose life would be ruined by alcohol.

The picture carries all the trappings of poverty that so bothered Thrasher and other critics. The brothers are at best modestly dressed. Although clean, they are surrounded by the grime that coated Bridgeport ca. 1918. It shows on the wooden wall and gate behind them. The sidewalk is also of wood. The boys' father did not live to ply his cement trade here.

In Chicago, slums and immigrants have always gone hand in hand, together with someone to offer comment. Nine years after Thrasher's book, the social reformer Edith Abbott finished a nearly five-hundred-page study of city slums including, inevitably, Bridgeport. Among the problems she found were "toilets [that] are located under the sidewalk. Here the conditions are worst, partly because they are so easily accessible to passers-by from the street."

The situation resulted from a decision city leaders had made in the 1850s to raise the street levels by as much as ten feet. The idea was to improve drainage for an area that, in ancient times, had occupied the bottom of a lake. Property owners downtown filled in vacant lots and jacked up buildings to install new basements; this way, entrances stayed flush with the street. In Bridgeport, only the streets were raised while sidewalks formed the roof over very dank vaults. Even today the neighborhood is dotted with front and back yards sunken well below street level.

Abbott complained, "Many of these toilets under the sidewalks are in such bad repair they are in no condition to be used. The water supply in many of them is often out of order, and in some instances toilet seats are broken or entirely lacking. Frequently, too, the floors are broken and damaged by rat holes."

To her credit, Abbott tried to avoid the busybody tendencies of other reformers. The people of Bridgeport did not upset her, just their housing. But she missed those ways the poor employ to cope with conditions resistant to change. Sometimes a few words strung together accomplished what the best documented studies could not.

My father had a saying, *Joe Podsidewalkiem*, the w sounding like a v. The translation is "Joe under the sidewalk." This was any Pole—in Chicago we sometimes refer to one another as "Joeys"—who was so poor, so unlucky, so ignorant as to meet nature's call beneath the street. *Joe Podsidewalkiem* was a tease and warning for the boys who played outside the bakery at 32nd and May: in Bridgeport you could end up lower than the gutter.

My father made sure such a fate did not befall his children. All he needed was to see me walking around the house with my shirt out or pants unzipped. That was his signal to say, "Don't act like a *Joe Podsidewalkiem*," sometimes coupled with the observation, "You smell like a billy goat." He treated his daughters the same way; pedal pushers merited the same attention as blue jeans. We had escaped his old neighborhood only to learn the same lessons it once taught him.

Abbott imagined a Bridgeport where slums gave way to public housing. It was a solution that did not interest my father. Thrasher proposed putting gang members into properly supervised activities. This was a future my father embraced without hesitation or doubt.

"A destructive gang in Central Park, New York City," Thrasher wrote, "was transformed into a Scout troop and given a cabin in the park for a meeting place. Vandalism at once ceased as they took up their new roles of junior policemen, protecting life and property." Thus could gang members be rendered into willing civic servants.

My father did not need a shack on the green for the Scouts to appeal to him. He gladly wore the uniform for an organization that infused his life with great purpose. As an adult he settled on a job that demanded nothing less than his forever earning a merit badge in firefighting. And what a clubhouse—with brass sliding pole and alarm bells to wake the dead.

During the 1920s his Scout troop assembled at Navy Pier to board a steamer, the *S.S. Carolina*, that took them across the lake to a camp in Michigan. This was another of those secrets that he held on to so tightly, letting go only in the last years of his life. The day before he told me, he had undergone a colonoscopy; usually this included the removal of several polyps. At the age of eighty-two he thought to recover by helping me clean the trap in my bathroom.

At the time I was writing the official history of Navy Pier, a mostly abandoned three-thousand-foot-long facility undergoing redevelopment by the city. Walking into the kitchen, he saw a Xerox on the table of a travel ad showing the *Carolina*; that triggered something to make him tell me. At first I was skeptical. There were any number of lake steamers back then, but a history of the steamship line proved him right.

The boys sailed on a great lake as their parents had crossed an ocean. Either way they traveled steerage, de facto or de jure. On the *Carolina*, first-class passengers could walk into a dining room for meals served on fine china with linen. Bridgeport Scouts were unlikely to join them. But they could see, and that may be why we used a tablecloth at home for special occasions.

I have a picture of the Scouts at Camp MacDonald dated "Aug. 24–26." The year is probably 1926. My father is sitting on the left in the first row. Out of a hundred or so boys, he cared enough to identify himself along with Bill, Chet, CHH, and Vince. His very presence in the picture means he had not yet been expelled from the Scouts. That happened when he tried to smuggle soda, or so he said, into camp. Expulsion saved him from quitting. He had reached an age where school and Scouts interfered with work.

When I was a boy, he would take me to a Scouting supply store on Archer Avenue, a few blocks from the firehouse. I remember we bought an official flashlight and pocketknife there. Other times we stopped merely to window-shop. Once, he brought home a few manuals. About school or the need to "button your fly" my father spoke freely, but the Scouts were different. Affection for something always chased the words from his mouth.

The best he could do was hope I would see for myself how the Scouts gave him purpose. But I never thought to join or to ask who his friends were in the picture or why he liked to wear a Scouts T-shirt around the house until the holes grew too big. He also bought a whistle with MADE IN USA stamped on the top of the mouthpiece. On the bottom was the Scouts' emblem of an eagle facing to the left, above the words BE PREPARED. When he found it lying in a drawer, he gave the whistle to his granddaughter, just as he had once given this gift to me. I found the Boy Scouts flashlight with red-white-and-blue banding at its base in a bedroom drawer the day after what would have been his ninetieth birthday.

*T*hrasher died at a New York state mental institution in 1962, when my father was forty-eight years old. The obituary in the *New York Times* reported that *The Gang* "is still considered an authoritative source in the field of juvenile delinquency." Apparently no one saw the need for a follow-up study to find how many onetime gang boys had escaped "demoralization." My father did, in part through Scouting and something that Thrasher wrote had failed "to penetrate in any real and vital way the experience of the gang boy." By this he meant organized religion. Sociology found it hard to accept Saul's transformation into Paul.

Thrasher was more interested in correlating faith and behavior. Catholicism had to be part of the problem if only because the city's leading gangsters were usually Catholic; Capone did have a way of causing church funerals. In the Baltimore Catechism, baptism washes away original sin. To Thrasher it was more a reliable predictor of criminality. He saw little evidence of the Holy Ghost dwelling in borderline delinquents or their places of worship.

My father's parish church stood down the street from the bakery. St. Mary of Perpetual Help called the faithful to Mass with its bells while always maintaining a viewable presence throughout the neighborhood; an immense copper dome rose more than a hundred feet above the traffic of 32nd Street. When my father attended St. Mary's grammar school, he was one of some seventeen hundred children enrolled.

Poles founded St. Mary's in 1882 because they did not feel comfortable at St. Bridget's on Archer Avenue; it was Irish. Other groups did the same. The Germans founded Immaculate Conception a few blocks away in 1883 while the Lithuanians left St. Mary's to start St. George's in 1892. This was the Bridgeport way: Out of Many, Many.

The faith that animated St. Mary's focused on a God who wanted immigrants to build Him great edifices in stone and marble while filling the pulpit with priests to reprise Jonathan Edwards, never mind the accent. This pre–Vatican II Catholicism made the middle child of a single mother feel both the depth of his sinfulness and the possibility of his redemption. It compelled him to serve as an altar boy and learn to say the rosary and pray novenas, devotions that ran over the course of nine days. Unlike his wife, my father kept his intentions private.

For years I saw him shower and shave a second time every evening for a week in March so he could attend the Lenten mission. The fire-and-brimstone sermons cleansed his soul of doubt. And for all his life my father received Communion only during the week or two following a visit to "the snitch box," his name for the sacrament of Confession. As much as anything, these elements of faith helped to gauge his physical decline and approaching death.

Following his first release from the hospital, Barbara and I decided to alternate weekends taking our parents to St. Gall, their parish church. We knew they had to partake of the Eucharist—and to see which of their neighbors could still handle the church stairs. For the first eight months my father participated as he always had, standing, kneeling, and beating his left breast three times with the fist of his right hand during the Consecration. *Mea culpa, mea culpa, mea maxima culpa.* He used a cane to walk up for Communion, and I took him to Confession every six weeks, though my mother wanted him to go whenever he swore at her.

Along with the rosary, my father often took a prayer book to church, the pages dog-eared from accumulated devotion; none of his other possessions showed such wear. At home he prayed on the back porch or in the living room, next to the lamp by his spot on the couch. For as long as I can remember, he gave generously to missionaries who worked with American Indians.

A month after his second major hospitalization, he began sitting during Mass. Next the cane was replaced by a walker, which in turn proved too hard for him to use during the Eucharist. Rather than have him go up to the front of the church, we arranged for Communion to be brought to the pew. Yet, through it all, he kept going to Confession, until May in his second year of suffering.

There had been still another series of arguments followed by phone calls from my mother that I take him to church. As her mind faltered, she was gripped by the fear that her husband's temper would consign him to Hell. By then I had a routine down, to get my father into the confessional and stand outside until I could hear the priest give absolution. The words "and sin no more" were my cue to open the door and help him out. Only this time he could not get up off his knees. He yelled for me to come get him.

The cry was so loud the priest stepped out of his confessional. Together we lifted my father to his feet. He sat in a pew, sweating and frightened by the way his body had betrayed him. After that, for the last six months of my father's life, a priest visited the house to forgive his sins.

The prayer book stayed next to him on the table by the lamp, but he used it less and less. He watches too much television, my mother complained. She was right: the freaks of Maury Povich and Jenny Jones had found a home in the living room. My mother insisted on exercising the mind and the body, even as she lost control of both.

I saw the fear from that Saturday Confession return the night of my father's last Thanksgiving. Ordinarily he would have gone with us to my in-laws for dinner, but he was too weak. We took my mother instead and left him with the new caregiver; someone had been living with my parents for the past eighteen months. When we returned, I went into the bedroom to look in on him. He said he wanted to get out of bed, which he could not manage alone.

Marija, the caregiver, helped me get him up and standing with his walker. Again I had to watch him try, and fail, in the effort to make his legs move. He sat down on the edge of the bed and began to cry. I waited for him to stop before calling in Clare, his only grandchild, to say goodnight. As they hugged, he told her, "Say a few Hail Marys so that your grandfather feels better." The next day I drove him to the hospital for the last time.

*M*y father believed that evil existed. Thrasher did too, in the form of a back-alley Satan: "Junk men sometimes actually instigate robberies on the part of the gang boy or his group—a direct encouragement to delinquent habits." While reformers identified the old man atop his wagon as a serious threat to public safety, few neighborhood boys would have agreed. For them he was Elijah, riding something far more practical than a chariot.

In Bridgeport, life was a zero-sum game that the junk man had figured out to mutual advantage with his customers. Together they found enough scrap metal and rags to make a little money. It was a more or less honest way to augment family income; if that entailed Ed Bukowski ditching school, so be it. He also picked through the alley garbage for bones, which he brought to a Stock Yards processor who ground them up into fertilizer.

These habits were handed down to the children. We collected old newspapers and bottles for money; with three empty quarts of Meister Brau in a bag, I was ready to brave Tee Zee's for the deposit. But I lacked his eye for salvage as well as his gift for making things whole again with a crescent wrench and screwdriver.

Twice that I know of he took home an old wringer washer that had been tossed away. Once carried into the basement, the machine did not stay broken for long. It was fixed because he disliked mixing work clothes with the family wash. He also walked the alley picking up aluminum cans for a neighbor's children to take to school; on visits I could hear him crushing cans in the basement. Retirement was a perpetual scrap drive for my father.

Shortly before I finished my Ph.D., he made a gift of three bookcases. Together they hold about four hundred volumes. Each one was crafted of wood he salvaged from packing crates at Wesco Spring; the stenciling still shows through the stain and varnish. Thus did the recycler of things bestow his blessing on the recycler of times. This talent of his was why my father held on so long, nearly three years, before dying. He had to be certain to use everything up and leave nothing of value behind. He knew no other way.

According to Mike Royko, "For a variety of reasons, ranging from convenience to fear to economics, people stayed in their own neighborhood, loving it, enjoying the closeness, the friendliness, the familiarity, and saving enough money to move out." Royko was, at best, half right. Our family never escaped Bridgeport. Only a *Joe Podsidewalkiem* would have thought to try.

As a teenager Ed Bukowski returned to the old neighborhood to attend a dance at St. George's, on Lituanica Avenue. There for the first time the shanty boy met the always lace-curtain girl. When they married and he brought her to the house on Homan Avenue, his mother moved back to Bridgeport.

We often went to visit her or my Uncle Doc. For years he had an office on Morgan Street, close to the apartment where my father was born. After work, provided my mother hadn't come along, the two brothers went out for drinks. They sat at the bar while I played arcade bowling off in a corner. A supply of quarters for the machine kept me from bothering them.

We also visited my uncle's house, a small Bridgeport worker's cottage in a sunken yard. There was actually a kind of gangplank that ran from the sidewalk to the front door. I remember Doc's wife, my Auntie Sis, always dressed in a robe, silk stockings rolled down to her ankles; she liked to serve cream soda. My uncle's drinking continued after their divorce.

A few months after my father's death I called the rectory at St. Mary's to see if his school records were still there. Several minutes into our conversation the woman asked, "Are you related to Dr. Bukowski?" My uncle, dead for thirty-four years, had done her sister's dentures. For the first time since freshman-year high school, Bridgeport made me Chester's nephew again.

Bridgeport stayed with us in another way. During the summer of 1919 my grandmother kept her children off 35th Street lest they be sucked into a race riot that claimed thirty-eight lives. Older boys from the neighborhood joined in the fight, perhaps Richard J. Daley among them, as his more unforgiving critics have intimated. My father was too young for that, three weeks shy of six. Under different circumstances, who knows?

The Bridgeport I saw as a child was cleaner and less crowded than the neighborhood of my father's youth, and less violent, at least for white people. Mayor Daley even recognized that part of his neighborhood where the Bukowski, Kropidlowski, and Skonieczny families lived together in the old bakery on May Street. They were, after all, good Democrats despite those difficult names. The mayor did not blame his Polish constituents for the lack of an "O'" before the avalanche of consonants and so allowed their streets to be cleaned and their garbage picked up.

The bakery was closing down by the time I began to anticipate our visits there. When we walked in, I would check to see if any of the trays had sweet rolls left. I also enjoyed "house cakes" baked in the shape of a triangle. Ours was a family of bakers, customer-patients, and dentists. The one called on the others.

We would sit in the front part of the store, my grandmother typically in her rocking chair. She sat beneath a clock that saw no reason to keep time quietly. In back were the white marble-top counter and a massive, gilt cash register; one of my great-uncles warned me not to get any ideas about opening it. These and other details I can recall, though not the words that passed between the old woman and her son. If only the clock had stopped ticking, just once.

The building itself was working-class Victorian, long and narrow, with a tin ceiling of geometric design. My father always complained tin sheets insulated a fire and had to be stripped away with a pike. I liked to sit out front in good weather and feel the cast-iron floor of the entrance grow warm in the sun.

I fell under the spell of Bridgeport at the age of eight. It was a crisp afternoon, probably a Saturday in early March, when I started off for the back of the bakery. My plan was to make it to the side door, where there was a chance someone might happen to see me. If caught, I would turn back without a fight. But Frederic Thrasher had left Bridgeport long ago, and the door stayed closed. My path to the alley was clear.

I had wanted to explore things in the way of any self-respecting Bridgeport boy; there was not supposed to be anyone rummaging through the bakery trash. He was what people then would have called a hobo, with a beard if not a bindle. For some reason he stopped long enough to introduce himself. He said he was from Cincinnati.

In that instant the direction of my life was set. I wanted to understand hoboes—another subject of study for Chicago School sociologists—and why the houses around the bakery had sunken yards and why the church down the street with the big dome looked so different from the funny green one I attended and why my grandmother's neighborhood sat across from cattle pens that had no cattle in them. Bridgeport touched me as it had my father. There was just one difference. I never shared in his poverty or the struggle to escape it.

We still visited the corner of 32nd and May in the years after my grandmother's death. My father's cousin, Doc Krops, owned the two-flat across from the bakery. He was one of my father's few real friends, and possibly his closest. To some extent it was a case of the prince and the pauper. I got to wear his son's hand-me-downs.

Doc Krops was Bridgeport royalty, in a non-Daley sort of way. He wore dress pants the way my father did work denim, and he drove a red Cadillac. His hair, combed straight back, exuded prosperity by its very length; crew cuts were for a different class of man. A successful dental practice gave him the money to move someplace better, but Doc Krops chose to stay in the neighborhood of his birth. He would leave Bridgeport when the mayor did, or not.

One Friday night in college I was hitchhiking on the far Northwest Side of Chicago. Technically it was closer to 2 A.M. Saturday morning, and I was on my way home after a night out. Not until midway through senior year did I own a car and stop taking my dates on the bus.

After a half-hour or so, a driver my age stopped and gave me a lift to the El. We talked to pass the time, which was how I learned he grew up in Bridgeport. He knew the bakery and Doc Krops across the street. "I hated those kids," he admitted of my cousins Celeste and Tom, "they had all the best toys." Doc Krops went first-class in everything, down to the tricycle and basement bar. It was done in overstuffed leather, the better to enjoy the champagne of bottled beers.

Sometimes we sat in the living room and listened while Doc Krops played the organ. Or we waited for him to return from bowling; the ball and carrying bag were his idea of conspicuous consumption. Mostly, though, we sat in the kitchen, where Doc Krops held court. During baseball season, with the windows open, we could hear Bill Veeck's exploding scoreboard at Comiskey Park whenever Floyd Robinson or Pete Ward provided too little too late against the Yankees.

Doc Krops excelled in the telling of stories. When the subject turned to war he became Richard returned from the Crusades by way of the Pacific theater. We were his subjects, still grateful decades later for his safe return. Before starting, he would turn to his most loyal attendant and ask, "Ed, does your boy want more soda?" I drank from the glass so fast the bubbles tickled my nose. There was no catching up once Doc Krops got under way.

He sat at the head of the table, the better to lead us: "We had a boy who liked to fall asleep without taking the hand grenades off his belt.

The C.O. told him not to do that, but he didn't listen. Then, one night he rolled over, and Boom!" His voice filled the room. Or it may have been the scoreboard.

My father kept a small portrait hidden away in a basement drawer of Doc Krops dressed in camouflage. His cousin is standing in a jungle clearing on some Pacific island. Doc Krops served, Ed bore witness. That may have been the secret of their friendship. Or Bridgeport itself connected them. They had both survived a place that others could but study and report on.

Doc Krops died when his cousin and friend was only sixty-six. As we made our way down the front steps of St. Mary's after the funeral Mass, my father turned to me and said, "I'm next." It was a pessimism that grew with age and infirmity. Grandchildren would have alleviated his condition, but he had to wait another twelve years for one.

I can picture our drives to Bridgeport past the stores of Archer Avenue, colored by the light of their neon signs, and over the river at Ashland. The railroad bridge, its girders blackened with the soot and dirt that once laced the air, still stands to the north of Archer. But most of the surrounding warehouses and factories exist only in memory or as a backdrop for certain dreams of mine.

Barbara, Betty, and I filled the back seat of the car on these trips. When we drove my grandmother back to the bakery, she sat up front between my parents. On the way home there would be much tickling and other forms of silliness. We might even stop for hot dogs. This was a world everyone in our family imagined would go on forever. I have more or less reconciled myself to its passing.

One of the Bridgeport photographs I have is of two children standing on the back stairs of a house probably a two-minute walk from the bakery. The girl is, perhaps, three years old, with a bow in her hair. The boy, dressed in a sailor suit, could be five years older. They are holding hands, like brother and sister. I have no idea who they are.

The other neighborhood photos are mostly of three weddings— or four depending how the pictures are grouped—at St. Mary's before my birth. The one bride I think I can identify is Alice. The others are just a guess. It's the cousins' picnic all over again, with people thirty years younger.

These pictures record the triumph and passing of Bridgeport, of the immigrants who fashioned a life free of broken privies and the children who are about to move away. No one knows yet how death will claim them. On a wedding day, thoughts turn to the future in a different way. *Stolat! Stolat!* May you live a hundred years.

Among the photographs is one of my sister Barbara standing alongside her grandmother. In another my mother is wearing a hat in the shape of a tiny ziggurat. Doc Krops looks very stylish in his two-tone shoes, and one of my great-aunts is wearing a fox stole draped around her shoulders. Waclaw must be standing somewhere in the crowd.

There is also a street shot, of five men aiming their 35-millimeter cameras in the direction of the church. I do not recognize any of them. They are strangers, though considerate enough to provide a clue to their identity.

Most of the photos are stamped on back with the name of a studio—Al's, Peters, Yank Candid. The interlopers were photographers working on spec. I remember them, or men like them, as a boy with my mother downtown on State Street. First they would snap our picture while walking backward, then stick an envelope in my hand with the address of the studio printed on it. A wedding made for easy pickings. What talent they had to coax smiles from people who did not usually take to outsiders.

The cameras were there the day my parents married on June 17, 1939, a Saturday. Albert Candid Photo on West 29th Street in Berwyn took a picture of the newlyweds standing on the front steps of my mother's church, Five Holy Martyrs, in Brighton Park. Ed Bukowski has made his way out of Bridgeport to the promise of a decent life on Homan Avenue. And he smiles. *Stolat!* The reception was held in our basement.

My father's funeral Mass also fell on a Saturday, in the first December of a new century.

James D. Hishen

Douglas on horseback

Betty with Mary Ann

III

ST. GALL

*E*very piece of real estate in Chicago includes a legal description drawn with the cold precision of a surveyor's instruments. The 5400 block of South Homan Avenue belongs to "Garfield Manor Subdivision of the South East quarter of the South East quarter of Section eleven (11), Township thirty-eight (38), Range thirteen (13), East of the Third Principal Meridian, in Cook County, Illinois." I grew up in the bungalow on lot thirty-six (36), block five (5).

Our street consisted of people who led simple lives with profound conviction. The men and women feared dirt as well as poverty; in their minds, the one led inexorably to the other. Children were raised to do well in school, wash their hands and face before dinner, get a job, start a family; as adults, they would live close enough to allow for Sunday visits with the grandchildren. The flag was displayed on holidays, weather permitting, from dawn until dusk. Everything would be clean, and nothing would ever change.

Hardly anyone said they lived in the community of Gage Park. That was a contrivance of city mapmakers, like West Elsdon, which began two blocks over. It made more sense to speak of Homan Avenue as part of St. Gall Parish rather than a park nearly a mile and a half away. Non-Catholics may have had their own name for the neighborhood, but such people were barely a rumor on our block.

I have a faded color photograph of an evening in the late spring of seventh grade, 1965. Families from around the parish are gathering to celebrate the annual May Crowning. By size I am a natural choice to carry the crucifix on a pole; I was more nervous than the picture shows. In church the congregation sings, "O Mary, we crown Thee with blossoms today, Queen of the Angels, Queen of the May." Even now the words of the hymn come easily.

A sizable crowd has gathered along 55th Street to watch as we march into church. The parishioners are devoted to Mary on account of Her generous presence across Europe, especially in Poland and Sicily. She is always welcome to visit the backyard grottos and statues maintained in Her honor. The American flag follows behind the cross in an ordering of symbols that does not strike onlookers as scandalous. Fourteen months later they will be more upset when civil rights marchers rally outside the church.

About the time I was in kindergarten, the parents of a friend three houses down—that would be lot 39—took me along for a ride to the North Side. We passed Wrigley Field, where the crowd had found something to cheer, and the Olson Rug Company factory at the corner of Diversey and Pulaski. The grounds featured a waterfall and rock garden. The company was so proud of the landscaping that it printed a postcard: "Here, too, are sparkling lagoons set in spacious lawns—the home of prize Corriedale sheep and hundreds of wild fowl." Factory-to-You Savings were yet another treat.

I could scarcely believe that anyone might live so far away— twenty-eight blocks north of the imaginary dividing line of Madison Street, as I lived fifty-four blocks south—and still be part of the same city. Through high school my world was considerably smaller, centering on a twelve-block stretch of Kedzie Avenue. It began at 5121 South in the second-floor offices of Dr. M. G. Farinacci, Practice Limited to Pediatrics. Asthma and allergies made me a regular patient.

The doctor saved my life one day in the fall of 1958 when my father carried me in choking from an asthma attack. I spent years being intimidated by the office photograph of Dr. and Mrs. Farinacci in audience with Pope John XXIII. It seemed sinful to complain about the state of my health.

Twice a week after school the doctor gave me shots that were supposed to lessen the chances of asthma. This went on six months of the year for eight years, beginning when I was six. Luckily Dr. Farinacci had his office above an appliance store. On the way home I saw Lionel train sets beckon through the display window.

My own train was bought secondhand. Family finances were tight then, and I have a vague recollection of the Eisenhower recession as that time my father was laid off from his hobby job. But birthdays and Christmas meant new rolling stock packed in orange boxes, like No. 3562-75 for the Operating BARREL CAR. During second grade my section of the basement began to resemble the train yard over on St. Louis Avenue. Lionel logs and barrels moved by vibration. So did our house ever so slightly, thanks to somewhat bigger trains.

Since the basement flooded nearly once a summer, nothing of value went on the floor. The train ran atop a specially built table, four feet by twelve feet, on legs twenty inches high; water usually stopped flowing out of the sewers after ten inches. Each corner of the table had crash walls to prevent derailments from landing onto the cement floor; this frustrated me while saving on the cost of repair bills. My father kept his love of gilt in check to paint the wood surface of the table forest green. He also provided the layout with a tiny forty-eight-star flag on a pole. Lionelville had to be every bit as patriotic as the rest of our household.

My father packed the train away when I outgrew it; then he drilled holes in the side of the table. With enough hooks screwed in, he was able to hang the platform from the basement rafters. There it stayed until he brought everything over when we moved into our first house. The Seaboard Railroad diesel and Santa Fe Super Chief were his idea of an aphrodisiac. I would put up the train set, then want a playmate—and he would have grandchildren. That is how it worked, factoring in a delay of six years and the appearance of just one child.

The train did not interfere with my after-school errands, to places like Minicino's Certified Grocery and Boulevard Cleaners, all located on or just off Kedzie. Saturdays I bought lunch meat on 57th Street at High Low Foods, a local chain. The store had a red-and-black checkerboard tile floor. I often roamed the aisles pretending to be an oversized checker piece; it was a game that did not seem to amuse adult customers. High Low also meant standing orders from my mother to tell the butcher everything had to be, as she put it, sliced thin.

Several times a week I stopped into Carl's, a small grocery on 55th Street, next door to Tee Zee's. The store was about the size of our living and dining rooms combined. Mostly I bought milk and bread or, when we ran out, New Mill Kluski Noodles.

Carl's was home to the unusual and unexpected. Smoked fish were piled on a tray next to the cash register; the fish stared but never spoke. Like me, they may have have been fascinated by the mechanical claw that snatched boxes of cereal from overhead shelves. Carl himself seemed to delight in Germanic stereotypes. He was short, muscular, and gruff. Our neighborhood grocer was also fond of cigars, usually butt-size, and meat-stained aprons.

Carl pretended to hold me personally responsible for the transfer of his hometown in Germany to Poland after World War I. Since I could not locate the port of Danzig on a map for the life of me, there seemed little reason to worry. The yelling was part of an always entertaining show. Where else could I see a classmate shoot craps for Twinkies, Carl coming out from behind the counter to roll his dice against the bread stand? Although I never told my parents about this, they were sure Carl's partner Mickey made book in the back.

To my parents, gambling constituted a serious sin. They would not be tempted by Las Vegas until retirement, and at the time Illinois had yet to legalize Bingo. Money was divided between the family budget and Talman, our savings and loan, located across the street from St. Gall. Kedzie Avenue rendered unto both Caesar and God.

Only the outside of Talman deceived, with sidewalks to break an immigrant's heart. They sparkled, but from nothing more precious than flecks of gypsum. Inside were murals that preached the virtues of thrift; naturally a likeness of Ben Franklin stood guard behind the tellers. "All things considered, no people on earth ever had it so good as we have here and now, in Chicago," read one of the ads Talman founder Ben F. Bohac ran in the newspaper. "How thankful we should be."

Talman offered pictures with Santa during the holidays (I still have ones of myself and Betty) along with donut holes and coffee every weekend. A musician played the theme from *The Third Man* on a zither in the lobby. Customers were thus encouraged to pick up "quarter savers" so that when the card was filled its contents could be added to a savings account, "OR, [to] start a child on the road to thrift and pride of ownership with a $10 dividend-earning account."

My mother made sure she joined the Christmas Club to budget for the holidays. In our family a few dollars put away in spring made a difference by the second week of December. I do not know to what extent, if any, Mr. Bohac engaged in the practice of redlining minority neighborhoods to deny them mortgages.

The Bukowski children all had accounts, with the expected supervision. We would learn, as adult customers did, to take great joy in watching new—and ever larger—account balances fill up the little green pages of a passbook. At the right time the money would become ours alone; for me that day waited until well after my college graduation. When our parents grew ill, we added our names to their accounts.

My father often took me along to cash his check, usually on a Friday night. Standing alongside him in line, I could see the care he took in handling the passbook; this was a possession, an identity, he would have instinctively defended with his life. On the way out he made sure to give a few dollars to the Salvation Army person in the lobby, as thanks for the refreshments that workers served at fires. It was all right if I picked up a copy of *War Cry*.

My parents used Talman for close to sixty years. They "went to the bank" (though it wasn't) to cash their checks, make deposits, and talk. There were always neighbors in line with them; money orders were a pleasant excuse to socialize. Nothing changed with retirement. Social Security and my father's pension merely presented new opportunities to save. Not even infirmity was allowed to get in the way of these trips. When my father could no longer drive, I took them. When he grew too weak, I went in his place.

*M*y maternal grandmother lived a ten-minute walk away, two blocks east of Kedzie, on 54th Street. I was the last of the three children to do shopping and chores for her. At the end of a visit she might invite me to go with her to Talman and share a few donut holes.

Like the other members of our family, my grandmother had stories from the Old World and the New. She was a product of the upheaval that seems to grip Europe with some regularity. In the late 1700s the Hapsburgs developed a taste for lands Polish. A hundred years later the peasant girl Ludwika pledged allegiance to Emperor Franz Joseph of Austria-Hungary in what German the schools taught her.

The second language came in handy when she made her way as a fifteen-year-old to the port of Bremen. "I knew '*kierke*,'" she recounted, "and '*eince, stri, dei.*'" We had to put my grandmother in a nursing home shortly before she turned ninety-six. During the last months of her life she marked my visits by singing hymns from her bed in German.

Louise Krawzyk Gurke always remembered the date of her arrival in America. "Douglas, it was March 22, 1902, in the port of Baltimore." I would be married seventy-eight years later to the day. But records put the arrival three days later. The discrepancy in dates should not be held against her; immigrants keep their own time. A government does not care if a peasant girl from Radomysl was kept waiting seventy-two hours for her papers to be stamped.

Immigration regularly blurred the identity of newcomers. At the very least, my grandparents were subjected to the rules of English grammar, not to mention the fatigue of government clerks tired from so much writing. A name known throughout the village for generations might be refracted into Gorka, Gurka, and, finally, Gurke. Between them, Ellis Island and the South Side could accept only so many non-WASP letter combinations. The survival of "Skonieczny" constitutes something of an etymological miracle.

Changes did not necessarily stop with the spelling of a surname. As Eras, an Austrian subject stepping off the steamer *Moltke* in April 1902, my grandfather indicated that he was a married man, though not to the woman who became my grandmother. As Ernest, he never spoke of another wife. Perhaps the ship's manifest was wrong, if only that would explain the other irregularities.

Ernest first tried for citizenship in the Circuit Court of Cook County. He swore, "I am not a polygamist nor a believer in polygamy," and he was ready to disavow allegiance to "Francis Joseph Emperor of Austria and Apostolic King of Hungary." That bit of Poland he called home had fallen under Austrian control in 1772. This was the city of Oswiecim, the eventual site of Auschwitz. Such is one of my connections to the old country.

My grandfather brought along a realtor–insurance agent and a saloon keeper for character witnesses. They were to convey a sense of substance that a man five-foot-five might not by himself. Still, the court chose to deny Eras citizenship, this on November 26, 1913. A clerk recorded, "The petitioner is an ignorant person." By that and the three previous continuances granted "to study Government," I assume my grandfather was illiterate. Or he may have let slip the story of being out late one night when two men robbed him and tried to toss him off a bridge into the Chicago River. It is never smart to walk around with too much money after having too much to drink.

The petitioner had better luck in Superior Court twelve years later. Then he renounced "forever all allegiance and fidelity" to the Republic of Poland; this new name for his homeland came about because the Hapsburgs had not fared well since his first try. Ernest swore again that he was a baker married to Ludwika (my grandmother), but his dates of birth and arrival in New York are all changed. Either he was up to something or the clerk was an ignorant person careless in copying down information.

The odd thing is that none of the discrepancies is major. In 1913 Ernest gave as his date of birth June 3, 1877; his departure from the port of Hamburg April 14, 1902; and his arrival in New York April 24. In 1925 his date of birth reads April 14, 1877, with his arrival on April 15, 1901. The one constant is the *Moltke*, a ship launched in 1902 and one my grandfather claims to have sailed on a year earlier, when it would have been under construction.

Grandma Bukowski had the same problem with her boat, the *Kaiserin Auguste Victoria*. She arrived in New York from Bremen May 8, 1901, on a vessel still five years in the future. "I do swear (affirm) that the statements I have made and the intentions I have expressed in this declaration of intention subscribed by me are true to the best of my knowledge and belief: SO HELP ME GOD."

In 1930 both Ernest and Elizabeth welcomed the Census taker into their homes. That person, no doubt happy to have even a temporary job in the depression, dutifully recorded the information given. Why would (s)he question it? Ernest again used 1901 as his year of arrival in the United States. For whatever reason, Elizabeth chose the year 1904. This all had to be part of some grand shell game predicated on the purchase of a steamship ticket, exact date unknown. If so, Ernest and Elizabeth were master players.

Even my Grandma Gurke found a need to stretch the truth. She often told a story that for thirty years I took as proof of her civic virtue: she liked President Roosevelt very much but couldn't vote for him. I think there was a bit of a pause in the first telling, just long enough for me to confuse Roosevelts and for her to add, "But I did vote for President Taft." I believed unconditionally because my grandmother did not lie. But women in Illinois could not vote for president until 1916, four years after Taft's second run. I remembered this from my own lectures only after I found that Louise took her oath of allegiance as a naturalized citizen in January 1928.

My parents were the children of people who fled a Europe of soon-to-be-former tsars and emperors; Chicago School sociologists were right about some of that disintegration they studied. The trip from village to port could not have been easy. Landlords and border guards stood in the way, as did the whole notion of emigration. A successful journey depended on the ability to do things on the fly: No, sir, we would never leave your lands untended; those are just some bundles of old clothes. Some vodka for your troubles, Herr Schmidt? Such a fine uniform you have on.

Improvisation did not always end at Ellis Island, as my grandparents showed in those court and Census records. Playing with the truth may have become second nature to someone like Ernest. For Elizabeth it was poverty that forced her hand. She countered death with a second marriage, desertion by choosing a son who could be counted on for financial support. Lies were told or the truth was kept in a dark place until people forgot. A family's survival depended on it.

My parents grew up in households that had made their peace with the social upheaval that attached itself to finding a new home. This my mother and father could not do as adults. So they accumulated an array of yardsticks and tape measures along with wood, fabric, saws, and pinking shears; these were the elements of a ritual to fend off the past. A new shelf or apron was not the point. Each cut my father and mother made indulged their need for certainty. The second generation seemed rigid only by the standards of critics whose fathers had not needed to dance around the question of bigamy.

To my mother, accounting was perhaps the greatest of all the professions a child could enter, something that demanded precision down to at least two decimal places. But I refused to devote myself to the pursuit of debits and credits in eternal balance, and dropped the one accounting course I took. My father wanted something different from me: to understand the importance of a carpenter's folding ruler. It was intended to mark life six inches per section for distances of up to six feet; anything further demanded extreme caution. I was not supposed to use the ruler for a toy.

The Taft story may or may not have been my grandmother's only fiction. There was another incident she often spoke of, about the first American she ever saw. He was a black man working on the docks. "I wondered what kind of place this was I had come to," she told me. It would make for an odd lie.

In Chicago she found work with one of the big packers, either Armour or Swift. One day a knife fell through a chute in the ceiling and nearly severed a finger. She carried the scar for more than seventy years. In the same way as Thomas, I saw it and so believed.

Louise would never be mistaken for my father's mother. She was short, barely five feet tall, and much heavier than Elizabeth. The wedding picture shows her as a bride more sincere than beautiful. And, unlike Elizabeth, Louise wore a gown. It was a sign of prosperity both current and to come. I was her favorite.

My sisters preferred Elizabeth. She captivated them while striking me as detached, even remote. In one picture she has bent down to put her arms around her grandson for a rare show of affection; I can't be more than eighteen months old. My grandmother is wearing a fitted coat and has short, waved hair. She was attractive well into her sixties. And there I am, squirming to break free. We were not the best of matches.

Elizabeth had made her way in the world with little help from any man, save her brother-in-law Waclaw. Since my parents raised their girls to have ambitions, she provided a bit of real-world inspiration. Louise, ever short and dressed in aprons, did not. But she exuded a gentleness that drew me to her.

My grandmother lived with her daughter Lou—actually Sophie, a name she detested to the point of taking a shortened form of her mother's—in the house on 54th Street. When my aunt went on vacation in the summer, one of the grandchildren slept over. Before bed, Louise liked to brush her waist-length hair in the bathroom. She would stop and smile on seeing me watch her. Other times I walked over after school if my mother had gone to spend the day shopping downtown. Together we worked on spelling words: Douglas honey, "finally" is spelled like this. And so it was.

A week did not pass without her telling me, "President Roosevelt was a great man. He made Social Security and two-week vacations," as in fact he had. Her favorite Poles were the astronomer Copernicus and the 1930s dictator Josef Pilsudski. The pianist and nationalist Ignaz Paderewski she did not seem to care for as much, though she bought an upright for my mother to play.

A Ukrainian suitor courted her in Lincoln Park with the promise of a fur coat. But Louise settled instead on Eras/Ernest, a baker proud of his fluency in German. My grandfather was given to drink, union politics, and the acquisition of property, if not wives. Five years after Louise left Poland, Ernest had her in a nice building he bought.

They lived on the Southwest Side, first on Maplewood, then Francisco and, finally, 54th Street, each of the homes a two-flat. It had not taken them long to learn one of the first rules of Chicago real estate, that rent can pay the mortgage. Louise and Ernest charted progress much as the three little pigs did—the first building was of wood, the second and third of brick. Together they raised five children. My grandmother also suffered a miscarriage and lost a child in infancy. When she was pregnant with her youngest, my Auntie Fran, the doctor advised her to have an abortion for fear she could not carry the baby to term. Louise refused.

Like my own father, Ernest showed considerable disregard for consequences. In Chicago it once mattered very much if the bread baked had a union label affixed to the crust. My grandfather abhorred the open shop in the same way the devil is said to avoid holy water. He chose unemployment over a nonunion job even as my mother's wedding day approached. She found it hard to forgive him sixty years after the fact. Senility has yet to claim her memory of him being carried home drunk when she was a child. How Mother yelled.

For his wedding picture, Eras sported a mustache in the manner of Kaiser Wilhelm. It was gone by the time he walked over to our house with that pocketful of candy. My grandfather's passing in 1956 gave me my first encounter with death. A day after the funeral I saw him standing in the hallway between the bathroom and my bedroom. This I imagined before the age of five.

My grandmother kept her house for another seventeen years, until her daughter Lou died. The grandchildren regularly supplied the labor to pick strawberries in the backyard garden or dig up molarshaped carrots worthy of Ripley's. The summer sleepovers were more fun and far less work.

There was a huge basement to hide in, front and back apartment stairs for spying on the second-floor tenants, and an alcove in the dining room for a 1940s telephone with ringer, WAlbrook 5-8442. The refrigerator was stocked with an endless supply of Jell-O and 7-Up for nighttime snacks. I stayed in my aunt's bedroom overlooking the backyard. The garden-sweet air of late summer made it easy to fall asleep. Not even the crickets kept me up.

My grandmother quietly bore the guilt of institutionalizing her son Michael. I may have reminded her of him before his illness. After moving in with us, she gave me a wristwatch that had belonged to him; it barely fits over my wrist. She motioned me into her bedroom and opened a drawer. Take it, she offered, and how could I not?

My grandmother performed a penance of regular visits to the state mental institution in Manteno. It was a ninety-minute bus trip south across the flat Illinois farmland. Once she saw a tornado ripping through a field in the distance. Still she visited, until age forced her to stop. My mother and Auntie Fran then took her place. I drove them once a month and helped draft letters to stop the state from releasing Michael to their care after more than thirty years; this was the "reform" of deinstitutionalization. My mother brought candy bars to her brother and asked him if he could say her name. "You should know who you are," he would answer back. Some days she can repeat this story more or less intact.

Buses were my grandmother's automobile. They took her to see what remained of her son and to enjoy the stores along State Street. To go downtown she would put on a good hat and white gloves before walking to the Kedzie bus stop. When the Archer bus dropped her at the corner of State and Washington, she stepped into "Marsh Field's," where the clerks were not permitted to distinguish between South Side and North Shore. A peasant girl could hardly imagine such pleasure as a pretty clerk's attention from across the counter.

Louise had an immigrant's devotion to property. One day in the summer of my sophomore year of college, I walked into an argument between her and a man posing as a contractor. He had gone up on the roof, uninvited, to find that she needed a new chimney. My grandmother was a mark who refused to be played. Douglas, go call the police. This became one of her favorite stories, if only because it gave me a supporting role.

Another time, when we were moving her to our house after my aunt's death, I drove up to find her kneeling by the front curb. She held a trowel in her hand. Workers who were replacing the sidewalk next door had given her a little cement to patch some cracks in the curb. Otherwise the new owners of the house might talk.

My father found it hard to have his mother-in-law live with us. She was the harbinger of an old age he wanted desperately to avoid. She walked too slowly, used a cane, and lost herself in the bathroom for up to an hour at a time. This premonition of his own future made him angry. "Lift your feet up," he would yell. "Don't drag them." But nothing he demanded of her could alter his own fate. Five years after her death, he had surgery for the removal of a brain tumor; the procedure left him without a sense of balance. That was when he began walking with her cane.

The two of them also shared a devotion to time. My father treated it with Old Testament regard—time made incessant demands which he tried his best to satisfy, no matter how little he understood them. For my grandmother, time was a gift to be celebrated, like her faith in Christ's return. The house on 54th Street was filled with Big Bens and Baby Bens, round or square, the product of Westclox in downstate La Salle. The town was close to where her son, my Uncle Charlie, had moved. He liked the area from his time with the CCC.

The clock faces shone at night as if by magic. Louise did not know about the women who ingested fatal amounts of radium from painting the numbers; to keep a point on the paint brush, workers dabbed the bristles on their tongues. Had somebody told her, she would have prayed for the repose of all their souls.

My grandmother carried a Baby Ben in her apron pocket. Periodically she fished it out to see the time. The hour hand never gave her cause to rush. I wound the clock for her and set it close to the bed at night, so she could see the hands properly. My father kept a Baby Ben next to him on the couch in the months before his death. He struggled to read it with hope borne of the New Testament.

Since I collect things, I took my grandmother's last Baby Ben when she died. For eighteen years it sat among other clocks on a shelf, until my daughter chose it for a spot on her nightstand. The crack in the plastic crystal did not bother her. Clare wanted something she could wind and see glow a luminescent green in the dark. Honey, take this one.

*T*he children in my neighborhood all seemed to have grandparents with clocks or vegetable gardens that needed tending. No one complained because we knew that good works brought with them some kind of reward. We especially liked the ones that came to us in this world. It might be a quarter for candy or an unexpected visit from the scissors grinder, who walked behind a small green and red pushcart. Those colors were meant to identify him, proudly, as Italian.

The ding-dong-ding of the bell signaled customers to get out of the house fast before the cart crossed over to the next block. I lived for dull cutting instruments that sparked to sharpness on the grinding wheel; if my mother couldn't find any, someone else did. A wooden slat fit between the two handles of the cart. The man sat on the board to work the pedals connected to the belt that moved the wheel; thumb to blade to stone completed the task. My father told me scissors grinders were always welcome at a firehouse. It was an exchange of services—sharpened axes for a secure spot to store the cart overnight.

Alleys were another source of wonder. The vegetable man drove a truck, the junk man a horse and wagon. Forces belonging to Richard J. Daley plied the front as well as the back. Despite the images of the 1968 Convention, Daley rarely used his centurions to enforce a harsh *Pax Democraticus* on us; he accomplished more with street cleaners and garbage trucks. I loved watching them both.

The street cleaner floated along the curb on swirling brushes to the excitement of anyone lucky enough to watch from the sidewalk. It was a high honor to find that your front lawn had been graced with one of those long, triangular signs announcing the time and day of the street cleaner's next visit. As for garbage pickup—here was a grown-up job noisome and dirty enough for a boy to aspire to. The "garbage men" expertly rolled, lifted, and emptied fifty-five-gallon drums, which were often a gift of the precinct captain. I was left with a respect for both manual labor and efficient political organization.

The unexpected arrived by way of the front porch. Brushes, safety pins, rocking chairs: people rang the doorbell to sell these and more. One day an elderly woman appeared with a basket of sewing notions. When, as a brusque thirteen-year-old, I told her we weren't interested, she began crying. My mother overheard and came to investigate; it was amazing the items she found to buy in that basket. The front porch also made the best spot for reading box scores in the afternoon *American*.

Along with place, Chicago could be a function of smell and sound. The neighborhoods all possessed distinct odors. On our block it was the Nabisco plant south of Marquette Park and cornstarch from far-off Argo; on Taylor and Western it might be those acrid fumes from the Acme Barrel Company. Everything depended on wind direction and distance. The Stock Yards were carried on a fetid breeze that, thankfully, rarely accosted us.

Our house stood two miles east of Midway Airport, a piece of Section 16 land dating from the Land Ordinance of 1785; airport revenues helped fund the Board of Education. Before World War II it was Municipal Airport. The name changed following the great naval battle of June 1942. Chicago has long honored heroes together with politicians. The airport also served a more personal use in summer. Thunderstorms frightened me as a child until I decoded Midway's foolproof all-clear signal. When planes began revving their engines, I knew that, regardless of the color of the sky overhead, the worst of the weather had passed.

After my Auntie Fran bought a new house (not a bungalow, but a "raised ranch") west of us, we had to pass the airport to get there. The two great, barrel-vaulted hangars along 55th Street loomed no more than thirty feet from our car window. Other times my mother and I walked to 63rd Street and took the bus to visit. Near the south runway sat two World War II bombers that had been intended for use at the Bay of Pigs.

Flight paths crossed 55th Street at Cicero and at Central. When we stopped for a red light, my father might suddenly shout, "The plane's gonna hit us!" He exaggerated by the fifty or so feet between our car roof and the plane's landing gear. The only drawback to Midway was size—Section 16 could not be stretched to accommodate the new Boeing 707s. At O'Hare we stood on an observation deck and watched passengers walk on a red carpet across the runway and up the stairs into a jet.

But airplanes were a secondary interest of mine, to trains. That was as it should be for a child growing up in the city of Chicago. We lived just two short blocks from a switching yard for the Grand Trunk Railroad. The yard provided neighborhood boys with the ultimate challenge—to sneak in or get away with the boast that they had. My friends and I were forever talking about the railroad "dicks" armed with pepper guns. To this day I have never seen the barrel of any such weapon.

There was no greater thrill for a twelve-year-old living on Homan or Trumbull Avenue than to sneak among the boxcars. They were fascinating to watch, massive and immobile one moment only to be jerked into motion the next by a diesel engine a hundred yards away. Or an engineer might send the car onto a siding. Steel wheels squealed on steel rails as the boxcar rolled along, to wait for another or for the laws of physics to slow it down.

I took very seriously stories about other boys, always with names I didn't recognize, who were "pinched" by the dicks or "hit in the ass" with pepper shot or lost a limb to a flying boxcar such as we saw. So I hid in the foundation of a long-demolished building. This vantage point allowed me to spy and well up with envy at the same time. I watched grown men play with railroads while they went about the business of handling the nation's freight.

One morning in spring a wooden boxcar appeared on a spur just outside of the yard proper. No adult followed to keep watch or post warnings. We then claimed the prize for ourselves, a magnificent toy compliments of the Grand Trunk. We climbed to the top, hid inside, used it to stage great battles in wars past and future. Then it was gone, and we went back to using the surrounding field for softball. Our gift never returned.

At times it seemed as if the house were awash in sound: Midway, the trains, a late-night drag race that played out somewhere along 51st Street. After high school the noise began to bother me worse than hearing cicadas in late August had, just before the start of a new school year. This was a different, more serious warning to South Side boys, that college would not let them return home to the old neighborhood and their fathers. Instead they would graduate to chase fine dreams that rarely settle on city blocks that go ungentrified.

But the horde of children along Homan Avenue cared little about their futures. For them life consisted of the immediate and the far-off, school and Christmas. I also counted down the days to late March, when the hot dog man appeared for the next six or seven months on the corner of 55th and Christiana.

His cart was a marvel of assembly-line efficiency: containers of tomatoes, onions, relish, and peppers lined up in a row, hot dogs and tamales (Tom Toms, with the girl on the wrapper imploring her companion, "Oh! Give *Me* a Bite") ready in the steamer. A propane lantern hissed at no one in particular as it bathed everything in a hard white light.

"Who next?" John always asked customers. He worked fast, using tongs to open the small stainless-steel doors of the compartments that kept the food warm; I breathed in each cloud of escaping steam. "Who next?" he repeated, and I was off. It helped that I walked fast and we lived close by. A block farther and I would have grown fat eating other people's food.

Johnny's corner also fell within the boundaries of St. Gall, which my father declared was "a League of Nations neighborhood." Our new church had large statues of Mary and Joseph on the walls flanking the altar. The dedication book called them "The Housewife" and "The Laborer," as were most but not all adult worshipers. Our patron was an Irish monk who lived far from the Emerald Isle, amongst the heathen in sixth- and seventh-century Switzerland. He was an inspiration to any Irish pastor who found himself assigned to a parish that did not elevate Patrick above all other saints.

In my neighborhood Poles joined with Germans, Italians, the Irish, and Lithuanians to live together without bloodshed or fisticuffs. Everyone had come from their own Bridgeport—North Side Jungles,

West Side Wilderness, South Side Badlands, as Thrasher divided the city—and wanted no more of the old ways. St. Gall's represented integration, Chicago style. What appeared lily-white by one measure stood out as diverse by another.

Our neighbors resembled my parents in demeanor and expectations. To them children were to be seen always quiet, disciplined, and busy lest they fall victim to the temptations associated with too much play. Two people in particular stand out. They were both immigrants, though we were more likely to call them DPs.

Everyone on our block played in the alley. The place that so worried reformers during my father's adolescence was by my youth transformed thanks to concrete paving and regular garbage pickup. While rats remained unwelcome, children were tolerated so long as they did not make a habit of venturing into a neighbor's yard.

Our fathers took their cars out of the garage in the morning and returned them in late afternoon. With the alley largely free of traffic the rest of the time, it was an athletic field of great convenience. No one minded the hard playing surface—boys knew that scrapes added character to their knees.

So we filled the air between garages with footballs and sixteen-inch softballs. The best players were the ones who threw deep and hit straight away. The alley is why Chicago never produced a quarterback adept at the down-and-out pass pattern or a great pull hitter other than Moose Skowron. Any ball that strayed into a backyard might be lost forever.

Some neighbors didn't care about errant hits and throws; others yelled only if we bruised their tomatoes. But opposite the Becvars lived a man with his hatchet. The gate was always locked, forcing us to jump the fence into his yard. If we dared walk on his grass, he gave chase. Any rubber ball that he scooped up came back at us in quarter sections. Our tormentor spoke with a strange accent, something other than Polish or Lithuanian. And he wore a green fatigue cap, like the Germans in North Africa; it all added to the dread we felt on seeing him. After my father told him off once, he made an effort to smile at me.

Casey did not have to force himself to be friendly. He and his wife moved in two houses down from us, when the Blahas retired to Wisconsin. Casey arrived in the United States a refugee from postwar Poland. He liked my father as someone who spoke his language. Our new neighbor would typically visit on Christmas Day, only to exhaust his command of English in a holiday greeting. He was also my father's barber. For two decades the cost of a haircut stayed the same: a shot of whiskey, with a refill for a tip.

To me Casey did not look Polish, if in fact ethnic groups possess distinguishing features. It is a weakness of Poles to want to pass for German, all blue eyes and blond hair, and this Casey could not do. He appeared more Russian than anything. His face was round with ruddy cheeks and eyes more accustomed to glancing west, not east, in the direction of Moscow; because of the times, he made me think of Khrushchev, with better dental work. But Soviet leaders did not have the tattoo Casey bore on the inside of one forearm, a series of numbers in blue. Our neighbor had survived a concentration camp. I never found a way to ask which one.

With children of his own, Casey might have posed less of a mystery. Then we could have traded secrets about our parents on the way to school. Or we might have tried to make sense of that inscription above the Kedzie Avenue entrance of St. Gall School: Teach Me Goodness, Discipline, Knowledge, O Lord. In practice those seven words translated into a mix of large classes, reading benches, and prayer. My class photo from first grade, Room Two, shows me as one of forty-six children in October 1958; Room One had another forty-nine students. We were taught by the Sister Servants of the Holy Heart of Mary, who practiced a life of faith through teaching. They had our respect and oftentimes our love.

It was the same for my father. At Holy Cross the Sisters of St. Casimir distributed Communion and counseled patients; fear often preyed on the elderly in their semi-private rooms. When I took him home after his second stay, we met a nun by the elevator. "I'm going to do what we talked about, Sister," he promised her. His face and voice resonated with a child's sincerity. "I know you will," the nun answered. Edwin always tried his best to be good.

My second-grade report card shows me absent for thirty-two days of school; it is a wonder I learned anything that year. Even though I was a prime candidate for retention, Sister Francesca gave me the benefit of the doubt. So did my fourth-grade teacher. Sister Jerome Marie actually saw in me the faintest hint of intelligence. She also ended a budding career in forgery.

One afternoon in the spring of 1962, a sudden thunderstorm at dismissal time forced everyone to wait until our mothers could come pick us up. Sister took that opportunity to ask about the signature on a failure notice; it wasn't hers, my mother replied. God or nature did me in. Not long after, I was pulled aside on the playground for some advice. Get the bat off your shoulder if you want to hit, Sister said. I tell Clare the same thing now. It is too bad the nuns have become a vanished people without a suitable myth or series of ruins to secure their place in memory. The stereotypes of movie comedy are a poor substitute.

At St. Gall the past was better shown than taught. Our history books tended to be old of themselves and not very interesting. A more intriguing story hung on the walls of the hallways. A group picture commemorated each graduating class. With a step to the left of the preceding year, familiar faces gave way to strangers. Beyond my sister Barbara, class of '56, stood line upon line of unfamiliar eighth-graders. I wondered what happened to them.

Our grammar books promised *Voyages in English*. I survived the shoals of sentence diagrams to learn rules for good speaking and writing. A speaker was always prepared, and a writer remembered one command in particular: "A sentence is a group of words expressing a complete thought." That rule has made it all but impossible for me to write in phrases and fragments.

During the fourth grade we read a short play, *The March of Good English*. There was Captain English, "the leader of the English Crusade," and his men the "language soldiers" E, N, G, L, I, S, and H. An illustration showed the characters dressed as conquistadors, armed with poleaxes. At the time, rules of grammar were very serious business.

Our readers comprised a series. Depending on grade and reading group (assigned by bench), we learned about our home, family, neighbors, parish, town, and valley. "Faith and Freedom" appeared at the bottom of the cover on each book. Probably none of us bothered with a back-page note addressed To The Teacher; we wouldn't have understood. The books were printed by Ginn and Company "In Accordance with the Educational Plan of Rt. Rev. Msgr. George Johnson, Ph.D. The Catholic University of America." I imagine the books reflected certain findings from a university-sponsored commission on American citizenship.

"Along with the acquisition of an increased foundational reading vocabulary," a pre-primer promised, "the pupil also acquires a further understanding of the first fundamental principle of Christian social living, namely, love." David and Ann did not merely spend their day in repetitious (word) play. "Through interesting story content, the child is led to see how God, the Source of love, manifests His Providence in the life of the individual through Christian parents and Christian home life." The readers made catechism, if not civics, redundant.

The students of St. Gall absorbed new lessons along with vocabulary. One book focused on "the beginning of social life in the school and neighborhood," another on the need for "active and cooperative participation in the spiritual and material functions of the parish." Each reader broadened the Catholic response to Frederic Thrasher and his cohorts.

Beyond the readers, I remember Mr. Smith in the fourth grade laboring to teach us Latin so we could better recite the Gloria and Credo. Then, in the fall of 1962, we encountered Vatican II, and so began the evolution of Confession into Reconciliation. We prayed the Angelus at noon on Wednesdays, attended Mass on the first Friday of every month, and were dismissed early on Wednesdays so the Catholics in public school could have their weekly religious instruction.

My education through eighth grade suffered more than a few gaps. The school had no science lab or gym, and the library was too small and in too warm a room to be of much value. The rudiments of phys ed waited until eighth grade, when the boys were made to run a mile in eleven minutes. It was our very own Bataan. After pull-ups—done on a pipe in the church basement—we were ready to scale the cliffs at Normandy.

I have often wondered why memories of St. Gall stay with me in a way that the rest of my schooling does not. There was no personal freedom to speak of; teachers filtered our intellectual curiosity through textbooks that bore a *Nihil Obstat* and *Imprimatur*. All I can point to for an answer is my first-grade class picture. There were ninety-five of us that day in October 1958. School records indicate that all but eleven children stayed to have their graduation pictures taken in the spring of 1966. That makes for an eight-year retention rate of 88 percent.

Part of the time we spent together sitting in the pews of the lower church to watch films on the life of Albert Schweitzer and the pursuit of the *Graf Spee*. The acoustics played no favorites. Schweitzer's piano could have been mistaken for the guns of a pocket battleship. Luckily the Christmas parties were held in school. Since our parish was blessed with two music academies and a school band, someone always brought in the accordion or violin to play while treats were passed out. Following a bit of Irish dancing, class was dismissed for the holidays.

We also sat together in church after school to practice receiving the Sacraments. With First Communion came our First Confessions. We were urged to remember that saints confessed no more than three venial sins per visit (either weekly or monthly, I have forgotten); even one mortal sin was out of the question. As part of our preparation for Confirmation in fifth grade, we took a daily quiz in class. I prepared by waiting to study until fifteen minutes before the test. Sister began drilling us at 9 A.M. The booklet stayed out of sight, resting half in my lap and half in the desk.

We ate a hot-dog lunch in Kedzie Hall or served it to the younger students once we reached eighth grade. We were devoted to Our Holy Mother and to book reports, the best of which won gold or silver stars on a classroom chart. The color and number of stars fueled our self-esteem.

We learned to be civil toward one another in class and rabid on the playground. During recess and at lunch, the boys played whatever sport was in season; a child soon learned to walk the playground on the lookout for an errant softball, basketball, or football, alone or in some combination once seasons overlapped. In seventh and eighth grades we played in CYO (Catholic Youth Organization) softball and basketball leagues to bring honor to our school. Losing triggered an adolescent sense of shame.

School and church molded us into a community of military bearing. Students at St. Gall always exhibited a discernible unit cohesion. So did our parents. It was to be expected of soldiers for Christ, regardless their age. My memories are those of a veteran.

In the summer before eighth grade I attended camp in Indiana, where a religious order rented out the grounds to our school. This was the site of another of my slight rebellions. One of our eighth-grade teachers ran the program. We did not quite see eye to eye. I didn't like his officiating, and he didn't like my attitude. After I protested a call in volleyball, he told me to go back to my bed if I wanted, which I did, for two days. I said it was asthma. War ensued with the new school year in September.

Mr. Eahart and I clashed over my knowledge of grammar, the new math, and this week's spelling words. If I forgot to stand while giving an answer, he made sure to remind me with his gift for sarcasm. He once invited the whole class to find grammatical errors in a sentence I wrote; when no one could, he called in the English teacher to point out a mistake with noun-pronoun agreement. What pleasure he took in ripping up my homework, and what mercy he showed in not having me do it over.

We also disagreed on matters of fashion. In March he wore green to my red. It was a struggle on behalf of patron saints, Patrick and Joseph, whose feast days fell within forty-eight hours of each other. Nine months seemed hardly time enough for us to finish our fight. I thought my problem would vanish on graduation. It never occurred to me that this adult was performing a service or that he had been hired precisely because of his approach to teaching. I was better at experiencing the dots than connecting them.

On June 12, 1966, Monsignor Hishen handed out diplomas which noted that each graduate had "satisfactorily completed the proper Elementary Course of Study." Such faint praise would not have stopped me from attending a parish high school, if St. Gall had thought of running one. Instead I went to an all-boys' Catholic school in unincorporated Cook County. St. Laurence was the League of Nations careening to September 1939. There in the lunchroom and corridors of E Wing, some of the old Bridgeport waited for me.

Where once we had been the children of God at St. Gall, we were now the young men of St. Laurence, good Vikings one and all. We lined up every morning on 55th and Homan to catch a charter bus that took us to school in Stickney Township. When the Congregation of Christian Brothers decided to open a twenty-five-acre campus, they found suburban land prices to their liking. The brothers knew the student body would come to them.

St. Laurence mixed a selection of college prep courses with large doses of discipline; any fighting between periods was strictly extracurricular. Students were ill-advised to adjust a window without first asking permission, or to forget their gym uniforms. Such infractions might result in after-school detention, which for some reason we called "jug," and with it the prospect of walking a mile to the nearest public bus stop. The surrounding fields turned ankle-deep with mud in spring.

We were to carry with us at all times a copy of the student handbook. This helped us to remember, "Discipline of the individual is basic to any development of manhood. Without discipline, true education is impossible. ST. LAURENCE HIGH SCHOOL effects a policy of firm and sound discipline that seeks to form, cultivate and strengthen the adolescent personality."

The brothers were fairly set in their ways. The librarian repeated stories demonstrating the courage of that good Catholic quarterback Johnny Unitas, before his divorce. Brother Jackson spoke of teaching Lew Alcindor at Power Memorial Academy in New York. He must have been terribly hurt by his former student's conversion to Islam.

Brother Murphy advised that the best anti-Communists lived in Spain and the Philippines. When we showed a lack of interest in any of his observations, Brother took to lecturing us on our lack of savvy or, worse, "perspicacity," his brogue climbing over each syllable. We called the very oldest teachers "walking holidays." Grieving was left for the next of kin.

One of the brothers looked to have been assigned straight out of college. He was unable to overcome his youth or the meanness of others. The young men of St. Laurence were little disposed to respect the quality of innocence. Rather, they did grotesque impressions of the religion teacher when his back was turned and sometimes when it was not.

Like us, Brother had to follow those rules spelled out in the handbook or our school would lose all reason for being. After a few months he made himself hit miscreants—myself included—on the palm of the hand with a thick piece of leather. Yet Brother refused to stop believing in our goodness. He wrote on one of my assignments that I had a pipeline to God, an observation about which he was sadly mistaken.

Racial prejudice could not be counted among the brothers' failings. They challenged the all-white student body to accept blacks as fellow Christians. All our lay teachers did likewise except for the drivers' ed instructor, who was not, in fact, a school employee. Students appreciated him for his easy manner and quick wit. He treated race as a series of jokes that in the company of adolescents were best left unsaid and unheard.

Of all my classes I dreaded gym the most. When our teachers were in the mood, they inflicted thirty-five minutes of exercise and relay races on us; that left ten minutes to shower and dress before the next class. There was little to recommend in such an activity as the wheelbarrow: a student walked to one end of the gymnasium on his hands while a partner held him by the ankles, then they changed places to go back. Despair lurked in the form of six-count burpies, a combination squat and push-up.

Dodgeball existed to separate the strong from the weak. By September of my sophomore year, I knew to check for anyone with hands big enough to hurl a volleyball the length of the gym. It was considered great sport to hit someone on the side of the head from long distance. If gym coincided with a lunch period during bad weather, the hunters and the hunted might perform before an audience grateful to be inside. A good kill led to cheers from the overhead bleachers: Yeah! *Panem et circenses.*

Our introduction to the game of dizzy stick waited until midway through senior year. We ran the length of the gym, put a broom handle to our foreheads, spun around four or five times, and then tried to run back. Some people slammed into folded bleachers, other people laughed. I managed to keep from throwing up. For whatever reason, this new activity never caught on.

Years later I used tales of high school to impress students in my twentieth-century American survey course. I showed my draft card, intact, and gave my whereabouts for part of the 1968 Democratic Convention—with my father at Comiskey Park for a ball game. Not everyone who fits the Baby Boomer demographic went to Woodstock in the summer of 1969. If they were like me, they walked the eight blocks to work as a stock boy at the Walgreens on 55th and California. Or a year later they followed their fathers into the factory, as my best friend Frank Trapani did a week after high school graduation, with no more than a hope of college in his future.

I finally put high school to rest midway through one of my lecture performances. At that instant the intent of those good brothers was revealed to me in full; why then and not before, I can't say. The student body of St. Laurence became draft eligible upon reaching the age of eighteen. With a birthday in late May, Frank registered that week he had off between the end of school and his new job at Dura Container, making caps to fit on jars of Skippy peanut butter. I followed on August 4. Mrs. Mazzia was kind enough to sign my draft card on behalf of the federal government.

A student molded by St. Laurence was a draftee who listened to his drill instructor. And the obedient grunt had a fighting chance to come home alive from Vietnam. That was the lesson first taught by Mr. Eahart and one I took nearly thirty years to value fully. My draft number had been just high enough at 112 ("Date of Mailing: Oct 27 1972" from Local Board No. 63 of the Selective Service System) to keep me from realizing this any sooner.

*V*ietnam was just one in a series of intrusions by the outside world on our neighborhood. For me they began in December 1958 when a fire at Our Lady of the Angels School killed ninety-two students and three nuns. Virtually overnight, fire drills were incorporated into our school routine. Regardless of the time of day or year, a passerby might encounter the entire St. Gall student body standing in the playground, a thousand children absolutely quiet as we waited for the all-clear to return to class or go home. Teachers did not explain why we had to walk down from the second floor quickly and quietly. At home or school, we knew to follow orders.

The Cuban Missile Crisis was played out during October of fifth grade. I remember one day just before the morning bell sounded. Ordinarily fall was the season to play with yo-yos and send our Duncan Imperials spinning Around the World. Fidel had other ideas. Several boys at the back of the line began arguing over which cities the Russians would hit first: "New York—no, Washington. Chicago for sure." We had no idea what we were talking about. A year later the assassination of John F. Kennedy found us all in class on a cold and rainy Friday before Thanksgiving.

The adults and children of the parish instinctively looked to Monsignor James D. Hishen in times of crisis. If he was unable to part the waters of Lake Michigan, Monsignor never made public that fact.

Father Hishen arrived as pastor in 1934 to serve the next thirty-four years in that role. While Christ built His church upon the rock that was Simon Peter, the Archdiocese of Chicago made do with its Hishens. Like earlier apostles, this one walked the streets of his community. Although Monsignor could not root out all sin, he made sure the worst of it stayed out of sight, indoors.

Monsignor Hishen's great joy—and, by extension, ours—was the church he began to build at the age of sixty. Hishen had come from Back of the Yards, next to Bridgeport and just as tough. It was a neighborhood of cops, petty criminals, and laborers from the meat-packing plants. The young Hishen made sure Back of the Yards included at least one dynamic priest.

He attended Georgetown before entering the seminary. After his ordination in 1920, Father Hishen spent fourteen years preparing for the day when he would receive a parish to lead for the rest of his productive life. He was a Catholic Burnham, with big plans, the most important of which had to wait for a depression and war to pass.

Hishen began fund-raising for the new church in 1954. The dedication book has a picture of the committee whose members solicited donations. They were the leading men of the parish, and we were used to opening the door to them. It was a little like the block rosary, when people went from house to house in the parish to pray a decade of Holy Marys. Now prayer led to a donation. Families were encouraged to give between $100 and $150. In return my parents received a commemorative plate showing the new church.

St. Gall balanced the ambitious with the practical. The foundation had already been laid in 1929, and a roof put over it; this was what we always called the lower church. Hishen would build a new temple atop the old, a great quarter-circle with the street side faced in polished granite and stained glass. The interior walls were of green glazed brick. They supported a ceiling divided into five sections, each a series of large, ridged plaster panels; it created a sense of movement over-head, as if the heavens were about to part. The church had seating for fourteen hundred worshipers, a figure our pastor always expected to reach on Sundays.

Hishen was made a "domestic prelate" and given the title of Right Reverend Monsignor in August 1957. He celebrated the dedication Mass eight months later, April 13, 1958. Any parishioners who had hoped for a more traditional design (the elongated Stations of the Cross could have passed for the work of Giacometti), knew not to complain out loud.

The parish marked this momentous event with a dedication book ("To our Blessed Lady in the Centennial Year of Her appearance to Bernadette at Lourdes"), bound in green leather with gold lettering. Reproduced was a telegram that must have thrilled everyone who read it: "Built by faith and sacrifice, this building stands as a splendid sym-bol of your religious conviction. Here, I am sure, you will be inspired to new heights of service to God and neighbor. Congratulations and best wishes." The message was signed Dwight D. Eisenhower.

Cardinal Stritch also sent his greetings. The two paragraphs at-tributed to Pius XII, including "Above all, try with your constant zeal to have all the faithful attend the Eucharistic Sacrifice from which they may obtain abundant and salutary fruit," were probably not done with St. Gall or any lay readership in mind. His Holiness would have been hard-pressed to find the archdiocese of Chicago on a map, let alone one of its 450 parishes scattered over 1,426 square miles of northern Illinois.

The church pictured in the book looks much as it did the day of my father's funeral Mass some forty-two years later. The passage of time shows in the other photos. Monsignor Hishen suffered from hubris of the grandest sort, seen from time to time on the South Side. Charles Comiskey once built a Baseball Palace of the World while

Monsignor wanted nothing less than a palace of worship for his people on Sundays and holy days of obligation. But it was not enough for him to show off a new church. Hishen wanted to put his whole parish on display. Adults and children posed for the camera as ordered.

To look at the pictures in the book is to behold a grand army of the faithful long since dispersed. Here are the First Cavalry, followed in close order by the Fifth Engineers. Music was provided by the hundred-strong St. Gall school band, which fed the community band, both under the direction of Otto Nagl. To this day I can barely distinguish between Nagl and Sousa; it is not a bad thing. And on page forty-two is the roster of officers for the Holy Name Society, with pledge. It reads in part:

> I pledge myself against perjury,
> Blasphemy, profanity, and obscene speech.
> I pledge my loyalty
> To the flag of my country
> And to the God-given principles
> Of freedom, justice and happiness
> For which it stands.
> I pledge my support
> To all lawful authority
> Both civic and religious.
> I dedicate my manhood
> To the Honor of the Sacred Name of Jesus Christ,
> And beg that He will keep me faithful
> To these pledges
> Until death.

The St. Gall Knights of the Altar, or altar boys, are on page forty-three. Among their ranks were twenty-two high school students, several of whom had to be giving serious thought to the priesthood. My sister Betty appears three pages later, in her Girl Scout uniform; she is standing next to an American flag. These adolescents were recruits in training, expected to take an oath of arms when the time came.

In graduate school I was struck by the hostility my faith aroused. Only then did I learn about the reactionary triumvirate of O'Connell, Cushing, and Spellman. The Catholicism of Boston and New York, I saw, differed from that of Chicago. Yet none of my professors seemed to know or care that we had Dorothy Day first.

Monsignor Hishen gave few hints to the schoolchildren that he too belonged to a decidedly Midwestern and progressive branch of the church. We feared him as a temperamental man who walked the hallways dressed in a black cassock with red piping. He also enjoyed wearing his biretta, a black cloth hat with the fabric gathered up to form a kind of Y on top. The resulting ridge allowed him to palm the hat whenever he liked; it was an impressive trick. And woe unto those who were caught talking in class during a visit from Monsignor.

Yet in certain ways Hishen was different. The church design he selected pointed to the future, not the Gothic past favored in Bridgeport and Back of the Yards. Our pastor also opened the rectory to visiting priests, regardless of skin color. Father Emanuel, from India, took a particular liking to our family; not even my measles could keep him away. And Hishen made sure that parish organizations did more than pray the rosary.

The monsignor came out of an extraordinary church environment. He was ordained during the long reign (1916–1939) of Archbishop and, later, Cardinal George Mundelein. Like Capone, Mundelein hailed from Brooklyn and brought with him to his adopted city a keen sense of purpose, which he applied to somewhat more worthy ends. Under Mundelein's leadership, Catholic Chicago sought to prove its patriotism through architecture and politics.

The cardinal made Georgian Revival the unofficial style for new churches. The faithful would go to Mass and Mt. Vernon all at once.

Mundelein also made known his preference for FDR over Father Coughlin. At no time did the cardinal have any use for Adolf Hitler, calling him "an Austrian paperhanger and a poor one at that." Unfortunately, memories of Mundelein are overshadowed by those of his contemporary, Colonel Robert R. McCormick, the isolationist publisher of the *Chicago Tribune*.

Mundelein dreamed of establishing a seminary with a national reputation. To that end he appointed a new rector in 1936. This was Father Reynold Hillenbrand, an adherent of faith-based social action. Hillenbrand helped establish the Young Christian Workers, Young Christian Students, and the Christian Family Movement, organizations devoted to making young and married Catholics socially aware. St. Gall welcomed branches of all three. In the years leading to Vatican II, Chicago Catholics could be just as informed on issues as the Americans for Democratic Action. It just wasn't a good idea to act without first consulting clergy.

The effect of these groups on the parish is difficult to gauge. No one in my family belonged to any of them; in fact, my father never joined the Holy Name Society or the Knights of Columbus. And Monsignor Hishen was no fool. He held on to the old ways for when the need arose. As pastor in the early 1960s he had the stature to call a boycott of morally objectionable films at the Colony on 59th Street; of course we obeyed. For us the world in and around St. Gall was divided into hierarchies that did not so much compete as complement one another. That was why another leader made sure to have his "greetings and best wishes" put in the dedication book, together with his picture. It showed a still youthful Richard J. Daley.

*T*he mayor was an astute leader whose subordinates waited outside church every weekend. They knew not to rush the Almighty. There was always time enough after Mass for the local Democratic ward organization to dispense favors: ask and ye shall have a tree trimmed or jury duty excused. The precinct captains usually took a spot next to the newspaper vendor on 55th Street. They saw us as their flock too, and we recognized our shepherds by their fedoras.

Daley and Hishen approached their work in identical fashion. Inside St. Gall were worshipers who skipped the collection basket, just as outside were voters who expected city services without strings attached. The job of monsignor and mayor alike was to separate the wheat from the chaff, the saved from the Republican and independent. If only the old nativists had come to the South Side in search of proof. Where I lived, the halls of government really did lead to the Catholic church and back.

My father drew the line at obeying Irish clergy. Politicians and fire captains he did not abide so quietly. Like Faust, he had learned that every bargain bore certain costs. Five houses down from us lived Pat Norris, who was already on the force. Why not you, too, Ed? he asked sometime between Bougainville and D day. My father could just as easily have become a policeman. But walking a beat would have entailed judging human behavior, something he did not believe possible outside of Confession. Fire frightened him less.

I found his training-class picture from August 1944 on a shelf in the bedroom closet. One side of the envelope is divided between a recipe ("Basic turkey stuffing for 10 lb bird," in my mother's handwriting, with the notation "do not make it mushy") and a list of names. "Bukowski" joined with "Callahan," "Duffy," "Enright," "McGuire," and "Sullivan." Nineteen men in all were trained by a team of Boyle, Gleason, McGurn, O'Connor, and Sheen. Fifteen years earlier this mix would likely have led to a brawl, with my father at more than a slight disadvantage. Now everyone had to be on their best behavior. None of the four rows had space for a black graduate.

A city job usually required a payment of time and money to the Democratic party. Whatever the amount, my father had paid off his debt by the time of my childhood. So we kept the precinct captain at arm's length, both after Mass and on the front porch before an election. The one exception coincided with my high school graduation, when I needed money for college tuition. The necessary arrangements were made for me to get a patronage job.

I was to do maintenance on the Chicago Skyway, an elevated toll road that branches off the Dan Ryan Expressway into Indiana. If only in passing, man and machine reconciled so that an eighteen-year-old could ride in the back of a service truck and watch the sun rise over Lake Michigan. It was a splendid view, framed in the structural steel of a bridge over the Calumet River.

The Skyway entrance ramp from the Ryan passes by Oak Woods Cemetery. This is the final resting place of Mayor William Hale "Big Bill" Thompson, whose career would take up five years of my life to research and write about. At the south end, the tollway offers a short-cut to the Ford plant on Torrence Avenue. As luck would have it, I maintained a road connecting the son's future to his father's past. This was still well before anyone saw fit to tell me stories or I thought of writing them down.

The cemetery with its lagoon and trees beckoned as an oasis away from the concrete desert of a city expressway in June. That is, it would have had I not been fired. Mowing grass along the entrance ramps aggravated my asthma to the point of chronic absenteeism. I lost my patronage job for failure to perform, possibly a first in the annals of Chicago politics. Somehow my parents found the money for school.

My father was a lonely man, made that way by circumstance and choice. Boys forced to work young have little time for friends and games beyond some Sunday football in the park. When he grew too old to play, even the choice of a team conspired against him. My father rooted for the Chicago Cardinals, a franchise that fled the South Side for St. Louis. If other fans learned to cheer for the Bears, he continued to mock Old Man Halas for his skinflint ways, to say nothing of those mostly sad-sack rosters.

My father followed the White Sox more for ascetic discipline than simple pleasure. Nellie Fox laid down the perfect sacrifice bunt, and Edwin Bukowski scraped together enough money to support his family. With enough effort, there was satisfaction to be derived from either act.

I inherited more than team loyalties from my father. There was also personality: his detachment became mine. I still wonder why. Growing up, I wanted to be popular, only for asthma to get in the way. Seven-year-olds have a subconscious fear of catching such things from a classmate. Or that child so wanted to be like his father that he came down with a sickness to make him that way.

Asthma encourages an almost perpetual self-sufficiency. Periods of good health are not to be wasted. So if none of my friends wanted to pedal his bike for an hour, I went alone to the massive overpass on Pulaski Road; it spans the Sanitary Ship Canal and Stevenson Expressway. In Chicago, public works and skyscrapers provide a bit of relief to a world gone flat. I coasted past the great red and white smokestacks of the Commonwealth Edison power plant at the north end or stopped midway to watch barges on their way to the Illinois River, and from there into the Mississippi.

Closer to home was a wetlands so old as to be called a swamp. The land paralleled a stretch of railroad tracks just north of 51st Street, a little over a mile from home. I rode over in search of frogs and fish. Someone had left behind an oversized pan for mixing cement that doubled as my flat-bottom boat. A few discarded two-by-fours made for decent poles.

My mother never learned to ride a bicycle. As her mother had, she relied on buses. Some Sundays we took the Kedzie bus to go fishing in the lagoon at Marquette Park. I carried the collapsible fiberglass pole and a can filled with worms from our backyard. No one seemed to notice such a child, or the woman in a dress sitting next to him. I was more impressed by my red-and-white bobber than the resident bluegills were.

The Garfield Express carried us all the way east, to within a few blocks of the lake, where it turned around in the parking lot of the Museum of Science and Industry. Once inside, my mother did not join in the long lines that formed for the U-505 and coal mine exhibits. She was the kind of person who liked to walk rather than wait. I was content to stare up at the ceiling, where the Stuka and the Spitfire hung from wires in frozen pursuit of each other.

I remember our trips together downtown as a source of urban wonder. We typically walked the four blocks from our house to wait in front of Sixta's Bakery for the Kedzie Avenue trolley bus. (Naturally, both my sisters worked at the bakery once they reached high school. Our kitchen never wanted for sweet rolls on the weekend.)

The bus that picked us up was leviathan, all green and white and huge. We pulled the cord that sounded a bell for the driver to let us off at Archer. From there we caught the express to State Street and stores like Charles A. Stevens, Lytton's, and Wieboldt's. They were places that understood my mother's insistence on style as well as value.

One Christmas we went to the Fair Store. Not only did Santa Claus personally welcome his young friends, he provided carnival rides at ten cents a ticket eight floors above the intersection of State and Adams. I don't recall any Christmas windows with the biting wit of Barneys New York. State Street drew too sincere a crowd.

On the way home we waited for leviathan outside the White Castle at Archer and Kedzie. If there was no bus in sight, we might go inside for a few of those small, square hamburgers peculiar to the chain. But the very best trips were those when the bus driver gave me a handful of expired transfers to serve as legal tender in a make-believe world. My favorites were printed on green paper, from the subway system I would take just once until college.

Neither bus nor bicycle factored into my most daring trip away from home. In fact it was more of a grand adventure on foot. Ordinarily I liked going with my parents to the Sears on 61st and Western Avenue. My father thought it wise to drive Fords and shop Sears. He also relied on the store's 10 percent discount for firemen.

The best part of Sears was the basement, where the tools and toys attracted boys according to age. If nothing caught my eye, I might walk by the appliance section to inspect the refrigerators on display. The papier-mâché eggs and pork chops were funny in an Ernie Kovacs sort of way. But that evening in the spring of 1961, I chose television over shopping. My parents had already pulled out of the garage, headed for Sears, by the time my program started. It turned out to be a repeat.

I followed after the car without telling my sister Betty. There were the four blocks to Kedzie, then another four blocks to California and a quarter-mile to Western Avenue. The athletic fields at Gage Park were as deserted as the high school. Still, I kept walking. I knew from my father to turn south on Western for another six blocks. But Western is one of the busiest streets in the city; the trucks and noise soon frightened me. It grew worse at 59th Street, by the American Can factory. Stamping machines with quotas to meet did not worry over the sensitive ears of a wandering child.

The car dealers on Western were in the habit of stringing little plastic pennants and propellers across their lots. The wind made a snap and whir that was hard to ignore. Any other time I would have stopped to stare at my reflection in the polished hood of some slightly used Buick or Mercury, but fear set too brisk a pace. By the time I reached the store, my parents had come and gone. There would be no ride home.

"Where were you?" my sister half-shouted when she saw me open the porch door. "You're lucky Mother and Father aren't back yet." They had gone somewhere after Sears. Otherwise the two of us would have been in considerable trouble. We thought it best for obvious reasons to keep the story of my walk to ourselves.

By eighth grade I no longer tempted fate this way. I asked permission before walking off to someplace like the ice cream parlor on the corner of 59th and Kedzie. Every neighborhood used to have a Gertie's, all plush animals and banana splits with samplers stacked in a glass display case by the cashier. Crowds from the Colony theater next door stepped in for a cone. My parents would take me after a double feature. It is hard for me to separate memories of *Ben Hur* from the aroma of hot fudge.

During their last trip to Wisconsin, I drove by the house on Homan Avenue to pull weeds. It had become another of the household tasks that no longer seemed to get done. Clare came along to help around the tomato plants. Afterward we went to Gertie's for a sundae, which she enjoyed in the way a child is supposed to when introduced to one of life's small pleasures. Our booth looked out onto 59th Street.

On a Monday night in March 1957, when I was perhaps a year and a half younger than my daughter was that afternoon, Alvin Palmer stood waiting for the bus directly across the street from where we sat. St. Patrick's was six days off and Easter Sunday five weeks after that. Police put the time of the incident at a few minutes before ten o'clock. Palmer could have been thinking about anything, of Christ's death and Resurrection, or the taste of his favorite ice cream, or the way a

CTA bus never comes when it should. After the ball peen hammer split open his skull, Alvin Palmer must have wondered, Why?

Newspaper stories said the seventeen-year-old Palmer was on his way home after visiting a friend on the West Side. He caught the attention of a group of teenagers (in my father's lexicon, "punks") driving down 59th Street. They were looking for someone to rob or beat up. Palmer died ten hours after being taken to Holy Cross Hospital.

Nearly a half-century before Palmer's death, a sixteen-year-old Langston Hughes visited Chicago from Cleveland, where his "best pal in high school was a Polish boy named Sartur Andrzejewski." As a youngster growing up in Lawrence, Kansas, Hughes "used to walk down to the Santa Fe station and stare at the railroad tracks, because the railroad tracks ran to Chicago, and Chicago was the biggest town in the world to me, much talked of by the people in Kansas."

Hughes found Chicago to be a city that captivated the descendants of slaves and serfs alike. "South State Street was in its glory then," he wrote in his autobiography *The Big Sea*, "a teeming Negro street with crowded theaters, restaurants, and cabarets. And excitement from noon to noon. Midnight was like day."

Hughes chose a Sunday to "set out walking alone to see what the city looked like. I wandered too far outside the Negro district, over beyond Wentworth, and was set upon by a group of white boys, who said they didn't allow niggers in that neighborhood. I went home with both eyes blacked and a swollen jaw." It was 1918, a year before the race riot. The passage of time, into a nuclear age, had not changed much.

Hughes made the mistake of crossing over into Armour Square or Canaryville, copies of Bridgeport in population and sensibility. Until cul-de-sacs offered a retreat out of the city, blue-collar communities on the South Side fought what they saw as the threat of integration in "their" neighborhoods. Simply to stand on a corner or wander across the wrong street risked violence. My parents often worried if they should let their girls go to Rainbow Beach, the scene of numerous racial incidents. When I tagged along with my sister Betty on the bus, there always seemed to be white boys who wanted to impress her by picking a fight.

Richard J. Daley had been mayor for just two years at the time of Palmer's murder. Daley owed his nomination in the 1955 Democratic primary to the margin run up in the most loyal machine wards, where the vast majority of black Chicagoans lived. While he was not about to challenge the practice of segregation in white neighborhoods, Daley understood that he had to move against unprovoked attacks.

More than 150 police worked the Palmer killing, which was solved within 48 hours. Among my classmates in first grade (two rows down and one over from me in the class picture) was the son of the officer who broke the case. Most of the suspects were rounded up at Gage Park High School. Although none of them belonged to St. Gall or even resided within miles, it seemed that, increasingly, their neighbors did.

White families fled racial change farther east to settle in our parish. My first-grade class of 95 swelled to a graduating class of 122 seven years later. This was not the kind of growth Monsignor Hishen had envisioned. During the 1950s in Chicago, an average of three and a half blocks a week changed from white to black. A regular topic of conversation at our dinner table was the "border," that imaginary line dividing the races. The closer it edged to Kedzie Avenue, the more worried my parents grew. "I don't know what we'll do if they move here," my mother would say. On our street, people spoke the words "they" and "them" with more emotion than ordinary euphemisms allowed.

The Archdiocese of Chicago understood that attacks on black people did not constitute the ideal of Catholic Action. Looking for a solution, church leaders prevailed on Saul Alinsky to work in ten South Side parishes that were home to 200,000 people. The neighborhood organizer was famous for his work in Back of the Yards, Monsignor Hishen's old neighborhood. There Alinsky had united residents by rallying them against big business and corrupt politics. He tried a similar approach as part of a plan that called for a 5 percent quota of blacks in white neighborhoods. Only no one wanted to play the villain, either as invader or attacker.

The changing neighborhoods were two miles off on Garfield Boulevard. This was not nearly far enough for Monsignor. He so much wanted to be like other priests at career's end, with time enough to bask in the glory of brick-and-mortar accomplishment. But our pastor did not have this option. At the age of seventy-one he was called on to protect the people of St. Gall, not least of all from themselves.

That effort led to a student exchange program between our seventh grade and a public school in the increasingly black Englewood neighborhood. It was all very civil, if a little awkward, as the sisters made sure none of the boys used playground language. A broken arm kept me from going. My introduction to the issue of race had to wait another year.

We graduated from eighth grade on the first Sunday in June 1966. Boys marched on one side of the main aisle in church, girls on the other, to receive their diploma from Monsignor, who sat on the altar done in white marble. But the pictures are blurred, and I can't recall the name of my partner.

I do remember we held the graduation party in our basement. My mother's side of the family predominated. There was my Grandma Gurke, my two aunts and cousins, along with some neighbors who dropped by. The food—Polish sausage, potato salad, Italian beef— went on a long table with a plastic cloth added for color. The workbench remained off limits to all but a few men. People shook my hand, filled their plates, and wondered if a black family might move next door. Now that it had found them, uncertainty refused to let go of my parents.

Martin Luther King, Jr., had been active in Chicago for a year already. In July 1965, Reverend King addressed a sympathetic crowd of ten thousand in Harold Ickes's old hometown of Winnetka. The next day he spoke in downtown Chicago, at Buckingham Fountain: "Negroes have continued to flee from behind the Cotton Curtain, but now they find after years of indifference and exploitation, Chicago has not turned out to be the new Jerusalem." Reverend King would discover that Chicago—most of all that part of the South Side I called home—was instead another Jericho, with more resistant walls.

Early in 1966 King rented an apartment on the West Side for his base of operations. That summer civil rights activists organized around a strategy of open-housing marches. They included two prayer vigils outside St. Gall, on July 17 and 24. My birthday fell on a Saturday, the 30th. The next day was the first riot in Marquette Park.

Five days later another civil rights march began at the park. Someone in the crowd hit King with a rock; the knife, however, missed him. At day's end the civil rights leader admitted, "I've never seen anything like it. I've been in many demonstrations all across the South, but I can say that I have never seen—even in Mississippi and Alabama—mobs as hostile and hate-filled as I've seen in Chicago."

The daily newspapers downplayed the early marches for fear of inciting further violence. This was one of the lessons of the 1919 Race Riot—that sensational press coverage fueled mob action. So the first prayer vigil outside St. Gall counted for less than the capture of mass murderer Richard Speck in a Skid Row flophouse. By the next week, marchers stopping in front of a church could be labeled old news and thus ignored a second time.

Coverage of the vigils at St. Gall fell to the *Southwest News-Herald*, a weekly delivered to our front steps every Thursday. The paper reported on the events of July 17: the remarks by Lithuania's consul-general-in-exile to a Marquette Park audience that his nation was being "erased from the map and her identity lost in the Russian empire"; an integrated picnic of one hundred people in another section of the park; and the first rally outside St. Gall. No incidents were reported at the church, "although there were some taunts and jeers by a group of teenagers." The second vigil was marked by egg tossing and more catcalls. Neither story mentioned my sister Betty.

Curiosity made her walk the four short blocks from our house to church for one of the vigils. By going out the back and through the alley, my sister would have passed backyards with a mix of flowers and vegetables in summer bloom. Leaving by the front, she would have made sure not to step on anyone's lawn. We were all taught to respect the property of others. This was why the behavior outside of church bothered her so much; no one was doing as we had always been taught. She told people around her that the marchers should be allowed to talk. At that point my sister was shoved and, I imagine, called a nigger lover. There was no one from the Holy Name Society to take her side. A church militant had broken ranks and fled before the enemy. In truth, that army was turning against itself.

The two of us drove to Marquette Park the day after my birthday because this time we were both curious. But I did not experience any kind of epiphany, or find out why people set automobiles on fire. Nor did I sense that these events were in any way historic. Incoming honor students at St. Laurence were required to read ten novels during the summer and take a test in September. My attention those last weeks of vacation was split between Marquette Park, *Lost Horizon*, and *A Night to Remember*.

My father had a saying that people "three times seven" were entitled to do as they pleased. Although his middle child was still a year short, he let her judge for herself. Betty was his favorite, or the one of us children most like him. He could have kept the car at the firehouse that day instead of giving it to my sister. I did not encourage the same level of trust. By my father's rules, only a clown of a son would want to watch such a mob. Obviously, other parents disagreed.

Monsignor Hishen had to wonder why his church was being singled out for attention. So did Archbishop John Cody, who protested to civil rights leaders that Hishen had been working hard to develop racial tolerance. He even hosted a meeting of area churches, Catholic and Protestant. The pastors drafted an open letter which ran in the *Southwest News-Herald* on August 4. "The violent and irresponsible actions of some members of the community threaten to destroy what we all cherish," the letter warned.

It continued: "We are not interested in having an all-Negro community, nor are we interested in maintaining a racially segregated community. We state as a clear moral principle that every man has a right to live in this or any other community without the burden of special restriction." This basic message was repeated at all Masses the following Sunday. With that Monsignor could do no more. He retired two years later and died in 1973. St. Gall remained predominantly white for another twenty years.

The violence that summer left the people of St. Gall and Marquette Park with a site-specific mark of Cain. Only those who stayed were labeled racists; absolution followed a move to the suburbs. My father never thought of quitting either his home or his job. Rather he spent three days fighting those fires that devastated the West Side following the assassination of Martin Luther King. But devotion to duty did not wipe away the stain.

Observers have long struggled to understand the behavior of residents around the park. As the violence flared, University of Chicago sociologist Morris Janowitz suggested that integration was too challenging a proposition for "lower middle class people, those least equipped in terms of education and social controls to absorb it." Philip Hauser, another sociologist at the school, believed the neighborhoods producing violence "are still in the process of culturalization and Americanization."

Neither gentleman may have known the extent of his school's contribution to the events they commented on. The home of laissez-faire economics and political science did not always practice what it taught to Nobel acclaim. In the 1930s and '40s the university funneled more than $80,000 to neighborhood groups fighting to keep the environs of Hyde Park lily-white. Their chief tool was the restrictive covenant, a rider on property deeds preventing the sale of a house to black buyers. When in 1948 the Supreme Court declared that such covenants were unconstitutional, the university found itself a bigger and better hammer. School officials were able to gain control of an ambitious urban renewal project covering nine hundred acres in Hyde Park and the adjoining neighborhood of Kenwood.

The plan called for razing nearly 650 apartment buildings with 6,100 units. The result was a community where rents now followed that principle so cherished by U of C economists, the law of supply and demand. Blacks faced the choice of paying Hyde Park rents or trying their luck in those neighborhoods to the west. An institution that had split the atom would be the rock while people I passed on my way to school or High Low made ready the hard place. Those were the forces that converged on Marquette Park.

Edwin Joseph Bukowski looked at the protesters marching down 55th Street and wondered why blacks couldn't be more like his family in Bridgeport. Richard Joseph Daley would have agreed. Daley once told a nun how, in Bridgeport, houses were "as old as on the West Side but the people took care of them, worked hard, kept the neighborhood clean, looked after their children." My father and his mayor both believed that blacks "should lift themselves up by their bootstraps like our grandparents did." Talking race, these two South Siders could have traded places, a press conference for our dinner table, and no one would have been the wiser.

It never occurred to either man that other people pulled themselves into exhaustion. That was made clear to me when the right front tire fell off my car. At the time I was juggling graduate school with a job in a wire warehouse while Daley was coming to the close of both his reign and his life.

My plan had been to work half a day and then maybe go to a movie. Instead my wheel drum came apart on the way home, at the corner of Jackson and Kedzie, on the asphalt apron of a CTA bus barn on the West Side. I had no alternative but to call my father, who was home early. A half-hour later he drove up to assess the damage. Can't fix it, he said. We walked across the street to a gas station, where he picked a telephone number from off the wall. He called the mechanic.

The problem was towed to Johnny Littlejohn, a blues player who made extra money fixing cars. He worked out of a garage on Fifth Avenue, as cruel a name as Wall Street had been for my grandfather Stanley. We were told to come back at eight o'clock that night.

The garage was ramshackle, with a dirt floor. There had to be blues records stacked on a chair in the corner. I would have asked Littlejohn what clubs he liked playing in, but small talk seemed out of place. The idea was to go in and out. The moment we walked through the door, our hosts (four or five middle-aged men with the dress and build of my father) made it clear the feeling was mutual. The conversation consisted of "How much?" followed by an answer. Ten years after the fact we were given a taste of July and August 1966, from the other side.

*E*ventually I joined those people fleeing to the suburbs. The fear of guilt by association was too much for me to bear. But I have yet to shed the working-class sensibility of my upbringing. The blame, or credit, again belongs to my father.

The factories I grew up with were a springboard to the middle class, the prize my elders fought so desperately to deny Southern blacks. When assembly lines began shutting down in the 1970s, the Great Migration slowed to a trickle. This change "saved" the area around St. Gall, if only so the children could grow up to move away and live in subdivisions with a hint of the English countryside in their names. Stubble from last year's crop showing through the new sod did not cost extra come spring.

My father passed along an ability to distinguish between "different" and "better." It animates the belief of mine that there was a way not taken, of clean factories staffed by a diverse workforce making useful goods; with a city committed to the ideals Monsignor Hishen outlined in his letter, there would have been a greater need for truck farms than suburbs. I do not yet understand an economy based on more new housing, microchips, and the constant retraining of human beings. At some point we are all old dogs in search of familiar surroundings. Anarchists chant protests that my father raised in casual conversation.

I grew up accustomed to the outlines of the world of manufacturing around me. The railroad ran north over 51st Street and east past Kedzie, where there was a roundhouse to service engines. Roadway Trucks operated a terminal at 51st and Homan, not far from the RCA warehouse, which stood across from the Central Steel and Wire plant that began at Kedzie. With the corner bars and gas stations added in, this was the manor to which South Siders were born.

Chicago business leaders played the role of robber baron to great acclaim. They treated their workers like peasants who had come to toil in castles wired for electricity. Large industrial buildings erected before World War II were usually constructed of brick and stone with a tower. The design separated the lord and his vassals from the masses, the front office from the production floor, as it proclaimed to the surrounding neighborhood, Here Is Work.

An industrial park stretched along 47th Street like a string of forts. There was another such complex farther north, on Pershing Road. This was where Frank and I registered for the draft. To step into one of the buildings was to lose all sense of self among the pillars and slab concrete floors. We did so as required by law or out of the need for a job.

My sister Barbara spent two summers in still another castle-factory to earn money for college. She worked at R. R. Donnelley and Sons, printers. The Lakeside Press was a massive complex two miles south of downtown, complete with corner buttresses on the tower; the architectural historian Carl Condit called the style "Gothic provenance." The Yellow Pages and the Sears catalog were printed there.

A few times my father let me come with him to pick up my sister; even he wanted company on occasion. It was a thrill simply to be out at midnight. I had no idea that bedlam might attend a shift change. This could not be night, I thought, with all the noise and the light that flooded the street from the factory windows and employees milling about. I was not prepared to see so much activity so late and so unrelated to play. Somehow we picked the Bukowski from out of the crowd and made our way home.

Donnelley announced the plant's closing in 1993, within days of Sears's decision to discontinue its Big Book. "We have no interest to linger in that location," said a company spokesperson. Neither did the firms along 47th Street or Pershing Road. They did not care that the older peasants had grown accustomed to steady work while the younger ones saved out of their paychecks to buy their freedom the way my sister did. There have been systems far worse. But this one collapsed anyway as the old lords decided to put the feudalism of factories behind them.

"We are not a food company or an apparel company or a shoe-care company," proclaimed one such lord who had embraced the new ways. "We are—and shall continue to be—a global marketer of branded consumer packaged goods." Black or white, the peasants be damned.

*W*ith offices on Kedzie less than a mile from Marquette Park, the *Southwest News-Herald* tried to make sense of the violence occurring just down the street. "Local residents have so much to lose and so little to gain," an editorial assumed. "Civil rights people have so much to gain and so little to lose." The *News-Herald* did not comment on missed opportunities. Perhaps it was too depressing, or, like so many others that summer, the paper didn't know quite what to think.

I refused to make of race what it had been for other South Siders. When Michele and I married, we moved to west suburban Oak Park, to stay for fifteen years. It is a community that prides itself on tolerance and diversity while drawing from a rich history steeped in Ernest Hemingway and Frank Lloyd Wright. But the village made me uncomfortable. On Homan Avenue no one ever thought to outlaw handguns or nuclear weapons. Of all the virtues on display in Oak Park, humility cannot be counted among them, and, of the virtues I need, that is perhaps the greatest.

Several years ago we left for Berwyn, a neighboring suburb and haven for bungalows. When the afternoon sun floods the gangway outside our bedroom, it reminds me of home. Most bungalows were built with only one window per bedroom. My parents had a view that looked out onto the front of the gangway, and the street. I had a view of the back, like our daughter now sees of the neighbor's yard.

But moving has made me restless. I keep thinking of Carl Sandburg with his Ashcan School of verse. Sandburg knew the bridge over the river at Clark Street, with its discordant voices of money and broken hearts. The poet-journalist heard a hooker in the courthouse on Harrison Street say, "I got nothin' to show for it. / Some man got it all, / Every night's hustlin' I ever did," and he challenged cartoonists to ride the Halsted streetcar. "Take your pencils / And draw these faces" of the pig sticker and factory girl, he urged.

Such faces were uncommon in Elmhurst, a pleasant suburb some thirty miles west of the city, where Sandburg lived from 1919 to 1930. Chicago's poet laureate left in the same way Richard M. Daley left his father's Bridgeport for a smart new townhouse development by the lake, or in the same way I left Homan Avenue. Only the fathers, Daley's and mine, stayed behind.

Pictures of the elder Daley remind me of my father. After his death I received a sympathy note from a friend. Even then he did not know how to call this man by anything other than Mr. Bukowski. On Lowe Street in Bridgeport, Daley was addressed by neighbors as "Mr. Mayor," though his biographers have preferred names like Boss and American Pharaoh. It is the second one that comes closer to the truth.

Daley did rule as king, however far from the Nile. He reigned over the city-state of Chicago, a modern-day Sparta with smokestacks. Daley was our Leonidas, and we followed him as subjects must; my father wore the dress blue of his army. Yet other warriors who hailed from our district served far beyond the city walls. When they had the time, these men wrote letters home that ran on the editorial page of the *Southwest News-Herald* under the headline, Mail Call from Viet Nam.

Then, in a moment of panic, we saw enemies where there were none, and the gods punished us for our mistake; they did not care that so many of us feared the uncertainty that attended the question of integration. My curse is to revere the story of Thermopylae along with the old ways while those around me forget. An old neighborhood's failings are the only memories allowed:

The parents of a friend of mine two houses down divorced when he was no more than eleven. A year later police carried out the father's body; alcohol killed him. Before John the Hot Dog Man spread relish on a bun, he might ask, "You want lilly? Fook-ee Lilly." It was his little joke. And Carl told me one of his stock boys liked to pull down the underpants of a doll sold in the store. These are all indicators of possible community dysfunction, sure to satisfy anyone already convinced of such a thing in such a place as I lived.

Pulitzer Prize–winning columnist Clarence Page has written that Northern cities were home to "white immigrants who received preferential treatment over blacks in hiring and union memberships, yet showed few feelings of guilt about it. 'Our families didn't own slaves' is still a popular guilt-cleansing refrain among their descendants."

Page means my family, from the sidewalk laborer and the union baker to the Chicago firefighter to me, someone profoundly ambivalent about the issue of racial reparations. If we ever gloated in victory or oppression, it showed in the pictures taken by an itinerant photographer.

He was a master of his trade, both skilled and anonymous; in another time he would have helped build Westminster or the cathedral at Rheims. His job promised a constant struggle with trees and clouds that kept the sun at bay. Sales were no easier. They depended on stamina and charm, ringing doorbells to smile over and over again, this block, the next, and the one after that, for as many days as life allows.

When my mother came to the door, they probably argued over price; it was all part of the dance. With a figure agreed on, he crossed the street to set up his equipment. The picture would be taken in a spot where the light was good, on the cinder driveway in front of Old Man Emo's garage. The hat, kerchief, and chaps went on me as they probably did another ten or twelve boys that day.

Then I was lifted onto the saddle, and someone, maybe a former denizen of the badlands home from work, showed me how to hold the reins. The pony was a good-looking paint, with a curl of hair that rested just above its eyes. So posed the smiling, three-year-old cowboy across from his family's bungalow on the South Side of Chicago.

He already loved Sparta very, very much.

Art on leave

*Family,
Christmas
1947*

Ed in the yard

IV

PICTURES OF HOME

There are places I remember
All my life, though some have changed,
Some forever, not for better,
Some have gone and some remain.
All these places had their moments,
With lovers and friends I still can recall
Some are dead and some are living,
In my life, I've loved them all.
    —from *In My Life*, John Lennon and
        Paul McCartney

*A*t parties people who hear me talk about growing up on the South Side assume by my degree that I mean Hyde Park. They either do not know or care about a crescent of development that stretched across the city. From 1900 to 1930, farmland and prairie yielded to the urban peasant's dream of a house with a yard, or did for my father and his family. The bungalow belt welcomed them but not others. It was a rejection that has been noted to the point of cliché, like Chicago made into a possessive of Capone.

No other American city allows transients to so define it. Even Carl Sandburg began and ended his life far from the borders of the place that made him famous. The result is civic reputation by patchwork, here a lyric in a protest song, there "a vast Canarsie," as A. J. Liebling wrote of Chicago after spending a few months in exile far from the editorial offices of his beloved *New Yorker*.

Liebling does not want for followers who would also treat urban history as the domain of New York—everything anyplace else is just local. When the boys came home from war, they soon left for Long Island, and so grew the suburbs. Jackie Robinson played ball in Brooklyn, and so began the march for civil rights. The New Deal ushered in social welfare programs that made Tammany Hall irrelevant, and so ended machine politics. If none of it happened that way in Chicago, the fault is ours.

The historian William Cronon learned to dislike Chicago while still a child. Cronon made annual trips through the city with his family on their way to Wisconsin. "The orange cloud of smoke was a signpost warning us of our entry into an alien landscape," he recalled of the South Side. The houses he saw from the car window were "always gray."

Cronon looked forward to the appearance of a huge neon beer sign "not least because it was a landmark showing the way out of The City." In adulthood Cronon admits to having been a willing "captive of the pastoral myth," though sad now for the wisdom gained with age and scholarship. "It turns out the green lake and the orange cloud have more in common than I thought." He discovered that country retreats were too often developed with the profits that emanated from smoke-belching factories.

In our neighborhood, nobody cared. Everyone, including the Irish, knew why orange had to mix with green. They were the primary colors of our prosperity, blending into blue and grey for the uniform shirts most of our fathers wore or the white that went on a sprinkling of collars. South Siders did not hate the environment, they just loved their jobs more. And, until the advent of sprawl, there was always a hint of nature around.

For more than a century the built city coexisted with the unbuilt. While never a balance of equals, it was a relationship all but impossible to miss. Conversations that began "I remember when it was all prairie from here" to some distant point on the horizon were more often based on fact than fiction. In 1889 Chicago annexed an area totaling 125 square miles, mostly farmland; this was the land that would fill up with bungalows. As late as V-J Day, a quarter of the city lay undeveloped.

My mother remembers the mile walk to school that left her and her brother Michael so dusty the teacher punished them for their appearance. My father remembered riding his bike past the fields that comprised the mile and a half to Municipal Airport. And I remember my Auntie Fran moving out of her mother's two-flat to a home just four miles away. There was a cow kept in a small pen by the railroad tracks.

Every generation had memories of an urban youth connected to someplace nearby that was "mostly prairie with plenty of wild flowers and cabbage fields." It did not matter that the flowers bloomed in Back of the Yards during the late 1800s or that Stock Yards workers on horseback chased after escaped cattle over the prairie there. This was Chicago in all its splendid paradox. An ability to see the "city's alienation from nature" demanded a level of skill few locals would ever possess, or care to.

The very oldest homes in our neighborhood were balloon frame, located close to 51st Street. They belonged to the families of workers at the Grand Trunk Railroad yard on St. Louis Avenue. Real change coincided with the advent of streetcar service down Kedzie, in 1902. Before that, the area was split between farms and homes.

Each decade the bungalow belt added new styles and ever more builders. Good times sped development by attracting newcomers like Ben Bohac. When he opened a building and loan in the kitchen of his Talman Avenue apartment in 1927, Bohac became a real George Bailey, offering mortgages to common people. They considered him an angel for it.

Chicago from the start embraced the Russian roulette of real estate speculation; it was nearly as exciting, without the mess. But not all speculators bought cheap and sold dear. Many overpaid for land, then held on to it for decades in the hope of recouping their investment. It is not uncommon to see a lot, still undeveloped, sitting between two seventy-five-year-old buildings. When the depression hit, everyone paid dear.

Construction stopped across the street from our front door. Between 51st and 55th streets and two blocks west, most of the land stood empty from the time of the Crash to just before the ascent of Daley I. This was one part of the birth order I would have changed. Both my sisters had a chance to play in the prairie. By the time I came along, the open land was nearly gone.

My mother ensured that her children did not run afoul of prairie or street. I always assumed this task of parenting demanded no more of her than it did the other women on the block. Then, at the age of thirty-nine, I finally became a father, and she told me a story.

One day Betty cried the way babies do on occasion, until all hope of sleep vanished. My father had escaped by virtue of the firehouse. The crying went on until my mother was ready to give in to temptation and do something she knew was wrong. But rather than strike an innocent, she put a rosary around her own neck, for strength. As a reward in old age, she began experiencing miracles.

The first one occurred in late 1989, on a Sunday afternoon in the dining room. Michele and I had come to take her to the hospital and visit my father. He was scheduled for surgery the next day, to have a shunt placed in the back of his skull for drainage. The phone rang as we were putting on our coats to leave. My mother answered. Unaccustomed to reprieves, she cried.

There would be no operation; the doctors had misread the x-ray. What they thought to be a buildup of fluid was in fact space created by the brain shrinking. It's a miracle, my mother said, and perhaps it was, because my father usually suffered an adverse reaction to anesthesia.

She was certain God assisted in other ways. Cortisone shots relieved the arthritic pain in her knee, and a night-light appeared out of the dark to guide her to the bathroom during her second hospital stay, less than two months before my father's death. God's handiwork did not stop there. My mother now waits to die in a house whose design is deemed "progressive" by decree of city hall. Even the pejorative use of the term "bungalow belt" seems to be in decline. This too is a miracle.

Bungalows are a product of their environment. Chicago lots tend to be narrow and deep, 25 or 30 feet by 125 feet. For decades after the Great Fire, builders invoked Darwin by the penny nail. Around 1900 a general design evolved for single-family dwellings: brick, one and a half stories, full basement, and hipped roof. The layout featured living room, dining room, and kitchen front to back, with bedrooms and bathroom off to one side or the other. This was the classic Chicago bungalow. Someone typically came along later to build enclosed back porches covered with asphalt siding.

Chicagoans refer to the narrow walk between houses as a gangway. The maritime allusion is intentional. A typical bungalow neighborhood resembles nothing so much as a fleet at anchor. This may be why St. Gall operated a Sea Explorers program attached to the Boy Scouts; members were dedicated to "life on the waves." Come July the streets shimmered like the lake off Rainbow Beach. And when the basements flooded, it was as if ballast had turned to bilge.

Some areas of the bungalow belt filled up with destroyers (two bedrooms, one bath) and cruisers (three bedrooms) while the battleships—octagon front (actually five sides in a bit of realtor hyperbole), leaded windows, and tile roofs—are moored on corner lots or fancy blocks. The Prairie homes of Frank Lloyd Wright, aircraft carriers by any other name, are a perfect complement.

We lived in a modified destroyer, with a third bedroom scooped out of the back half of the attic. My sisters slept there first, and, after my grandmother moved in, so did I. Our house provided shelter from all weather extremes. The atomic blast at Bikini Atoll would have caused little damage to a group of Chicago bungalows. Comfort was another matter.

The problem is that, come June, brick takes on the properties of a kiln or a ship straddling the equator. With air conditioning a luxury beyond our means until I reached college, the summer heat visited in two waves, day and night. One-window bedrooms begat boiler rooms, or so it seemed, to the point that summer nearly made a virtue of January.

One way to escape the heat was to set up a basement flat, with buckets on hand in case of flooding. This idea worked so well, at least in dry years, that more than a few people moved into the basement full-time; they ventured upstairs only for company, if that. Thankfully, my parents compromised. They put a gas stove downstairs to prepare meals in summer while staying upstairs year round. We coped with the heat in other ways—by eating supper on the back porch or dragging mattresses to sleep on into the living room. That was how I stayed up late to watch Steve Allen do *The Tonight Show*.

Of the winter months, February was the most likely to leave a mark. Slightly rising temperatures created the "good packing" necessary for snowball fights. After school ten or more boys would line up against an equal number, with the street between them. The fight continued until sundown or until an adult walked out on the front porch to chase everyone away. Battlefields included dozens of icy bumps adhering to pavement, sidewalk, and brick. Where snowball touched skin, it showed red.

Whatever the season, our block rivaled the activity of a shipyard in wartime. Coal bins were ripped out to be replaced by natural gas furnaces; attics were made into extra bedrooms (where sloping ceilings ran into unsuspecting foreheads). Attention also was paid to the bungalow "keel" stretching the length of a basement ceiling. Actually it is three timber beams supported by posts to carry the weight of the house. My father arranged to have the wooden support posts replaced with steel ones in the same way he replaced stairs, sidewalks, and fences or built a garage. The neighborhood armada was forever upgrading.

The golden age of the bungalow (I now live in a neighborhood that realtors call the Gold Coast of Berwyn) ended with the Crash. By then some eighty thousand bungalows spread over metropolitan Chicago. According to my father, our house was purchased from the builder, Julius Szabo. His likes are not to be found anymore in the Saturday real estate section. Mr. Szabo was an independent. He bought some lots, put up a few homes, and moved on. The bungalow belt is the legacy of hundreds of Szabos.

Bungalows are not assembly-line housing, as it is sometimes said. Henry Ford would have gone mad trying to accommodate the variety of attic stairs alone. In our house they were located in a corner of the kitchen, steep and with a mean corkscrew turn at the bottom. My sister Barbara tripped coming down them the morning of her wedding. She went to church dazed, though nothing was broken.

So I grew up thinking everyone had attic stairs in the kitchen. Then I moved into an Oak Park bungalow with stairs in the hallway. It was a minor shock that took some getting used to. Next came a child of my own and the two-year search for yet another bungalow; the habit of living in one is hard to break. Weekend open houses revealed attic stairs in the dining room, on the back porch, and in bedrooms. The last qualified as ingenious or perverse, depending on age. A layout that allowed parents to sleep at the foot of the stairs to an attic bedroom did not bode well for children on late dates.

The charms of a bungalow can be found in features as simple as a built-in ironing board. Our kitchen had two, regular sized and a small one above for sleeves; they folded up to rest behind a narrow oak door. With the ironing boards removed, the space can be reworked into a spice rack.

Face brick requires no alteration. Neighboring bungalows rarely if ever come with exactly the same brick in front. It can be smooth or lined vertically or both, set in such patterns as herringbone and checkerboard, with colors ranging from tan to black. The face brick on our house was a textured reddish brown, like frosting. Only corner bungalows have face brick on both street sides. That was a sign of real status in the neighborhood. A house entirely of face brick signaled wealth beyond comprehension.

New houses don't utilize limestone the way bungalows did, for the front porch and window sills and the brackets to hold flower boxes. Limestone quoins along with the occasional square or diamond above the front windows existed simply to delight the eye. Mies would not have tolerated such a violation of function, but he was not known to visit our street.

The attic dormers are another distinguishing feature. They come hipped, notched, and gabled, with two windows or three. And so it went, with front doors that differed, and windows and shingles. There was no need of ticky tack in the bungalow belt.

Whether or not he read them, Mr. Szabo built in the spirit of Ruskin and Morris. His homes embodied the ideals of simplicity, virtue, and beauty. The living room featured mantel and hearth, the warmth provided by gas jets rather than logs; rooms were banded floor and ceiling in oak; and the bedrooms provided a bit of privacy between brother and sisters. My first memory of leaded glass is the window in my parents' closet, which looks out onto the front porch. It has a simple T design, the letter (or is it a cross?) in green against a background of light yellow.

Original front porches on a bungalow have stairs flanked by brick walls topped with slabs of limestone. The walls come in one of two designs, as if two giant steps or angled in the manner of a slide; we had the first, my Grandma Gurke the second. The two walls of the porch proper extend about waist high. These are also topped with limestone.

Once, as a nine-year-old, I went to the hardware store for a small bottle of Testor's orange paint to mark the helmets of my toy soldiers; a friend had already done his army in brown. I gathered my forces on the porch only to spill the paint on the limestone. After more than forty years the stain still shows. The limestone tops on the porch and stair walls of a bungalow make perfect platforms for leaping or posing. Broken bones and pictures have happened there.

The porch provided cover during snowball fights and games of war. Later my friends and I sat at the top of the stairs playing Strat-O-Matic Baseball. We spent the summers of 1966–1968 in a ritual of throwing dice with one hand while clutching our player cards in the other. Queequeg could not have been any more intense kneeling on the deck of the *Pequod*. But we did not know to be literary stoics. A bad roll of the dice turned us into young Leo Durochers. Open windows and adult ears tended to cut short our imitations of The Lip, who was then managing the Cubs.

My parents used the front porch in all sorts of photographs. The oldest one I have shows my mother sitting on the limestone top of the porch wall; her feet are resting on the limestone of the north stair wall. My guess would be that the scene dates to just before or after she married. The early snapshots have decorative borders; the one of her holding baby Barbara in the fall of 1942 does not. So the picture border, which looks a little like Kilroy with his nose cut off, indicates this is Mary Ann Bukowski, nee Gurke, on or about June 1939.

She has on a dark dress with embroidered collar. She is smiling in that demure manner of hers and wearing heels. Her feet went bad sometime in the 1980s. That was when she switched to flats and pants. People continued to complement my mother on her youthful good looks, but she resented every concession to age no less than my father did.

The porch together with the front lawn served as our family altar. This was the place where my parents offered up their children, through a lens to God. The picture of my mother with Barbara on the porch is a double exposure, two scenes of a woman cradling her first-born so very carefully. The same role of film—that is, both pictures are stamped "570"—includes two shots of my father with his baby girl. His left arm supports her infant legs while his right holds her back and head; this was the same man who wielded a sledgehammer to break old concrete in the gangway. All the pictures are bathed in shadow. Only adult and child stand out, along with a portion of the closet window. I'm sure now the design shows a cross.

There are just a few baby pictures of Betty out front, which would seem to confirm her status as the nearly forgotten middle child. But they do include the all-important First Communion, where a happy girl dressed all in white stands alongside her proud mother, who wore pearls that day. Behind them, on the northwest corner of 54th and Homan, stands a building under construction. In the language of the neighborhood, it is not a bungalow but a "new house," postwar, and not to be confused with a "frame house" made of wood.

My sisters still complain that I was the favorite child, both the first boy and the last born. I can imagine them pointing out pictures of me on the front stairs in my Little League uniform or sitting between my father and an oversized kite. This was the time we went over to the railroad tracks on St. Louis; I was wearing an old blue sweatshirt my mother could not get me to throw away. The wind died all at once, and the kite landed in an open gondola car. My father got dirty retrieving our Hi-Flyer; the coal dust shows on his knees. But I never played "league" growing up or flew a kite in the spring. The March wind aggravated my asthma.

The pictures that do exist of me outside with my father are not among my favorites. As with Barbara, he holds his baby on the porch, only 1942 has passed. Obviously my father is ten years older and more than thirty pounds heavier. There is another difference. The infant with tousled knit cap does not elicit that same look of devotion, or so I think. It's the same with a snapshot from a year later, in the summer of 1953.

My father is wearing a short-sleeved shirt with lattice, diamond, and flower print colored a beer-bottle brown. He kept the shirt for years, long enough for me to remember clearly. I am sitting on his thigh like a ventriloquist's dummy, pinned to the massive chest by a calloused hand. Neither of us appears very happy, as if this was the first time he called me helpless and the first time I understood. Maybe it was the heat that made us look so uncomfortable.

I am much better at interpreting pictures showing my sisters, who seem to have spent a good deal of time in front of the house. There is a four-year age difference between them. Born in August 1942, Barbara was a war baby. Coming four years later, Betty was an early Boomer. The outline of their relationship is detailed in three photos.

The first must have been taken within months of Betty's birth in May 1946. Sitting on a small chair, Barbara struggles to keep the baby on her lap. Even at that early age, our big sister refuses to admit defeat. In the other two snapshots, the sisters are holding hands. As the older child, Barbara appears to be the one in control. She would have told little Betty to stand straight and smile, just as she now asks her to mix a vodka gimlet.

Had she been born a decade later, Barbara might easily have made the decision to go to medical school. She was gifted in science and helped me through equations in freshman-year algebra at St. Laurence. But our family physician told my mother, No, women were better suited as nurses. The doctor meant well, and under the circumstances may have been right. My parents had three children to budget for, not one. It was enough that their eldest be the first among her girl cousins to go to college. Barbara did not try to change anyone's mind; we all accepted the need for obedience. But my sister has a personality that allows her to work with others only on an equal basis. This led her to choose pharmacy over nursing. My sister joined a profession that would beat back the illnesses of old age, one of the greatest of all earthly powers, with a volley of pills. It was not a fair fight.

Everyone's attention returned to the eldest child. She had been the one to win scholarships and baby-sit siblings. It was now time for her to help out again. Suddenly she had to decide which medications her father would take, what foods he should eat, whether he could drive again. This was the burden of being first, an accident of birth that did not permit escape. For more than two years Barbara struggled to find the right formula to make him well. My parents' refrigerator was turned into a Polish delicatessen on the chance that duck blood soup together with *kolachki* could effect a cure. The kitchen counter doubled as a dispensary.

If she happened across a promising new drug at work, Barbara made sure the doctor wrote a prescription for her father. She brought the medicine over and added it to the mix; there came to be pills for morning, noon, evening, and night. Then she would stop by with groceries to ask, "Dad, how do you feel?" and he would answer, "Punk." It was not supposed to work that way. Daddy's big girl hated to disappoint him.

Barbara also posed out front on her First Communion, sausage curls showing under the veil. The curls were gone by the time of the eighth-grade graduation picture. My big sister is very serious, and a little stocky. Four years later the young woman leaving Visitation High School bound for the University of Illinois at Navy Pier—where seagulls squawked outside the windows during lectures—is striking, thinner now and tall, with full lips. The look of confidence becomes her. Only my father's illness and death will alter it.

The picture of my parents standing outside the house dates to July 1960, when they were a month short of forty-seven. In the background is the front porch, my father's latest project: he has ripped out the stairs and flanking walls, poured new concrete, and installed railings on either side. This had to occupy him for a month minimum. The postman was left to figure out a way to deliver our mail.

Of the two, it is my father who looks older, with receding hairline and a frame that has filled out to being stout; my mother is wearing pearls and matching earrings. It is something of a miracle that they are standing together. By this time one of them should be living with me in Arizona.

My health as a child was miserable. By the age of five I had been diagnosed with severe asthma. It came with October and lasted through the cold weather, which for Chicago can mean April or May. In the autumn of first grade I suffered an attack that literally turned me blue. My father rushed home from the firehouse and brought me to Dr. Farinacci, who administered a shot of adrenalin before I suffocated. That was followed by two weeks in the hospital, five days spent under an oxygen tent. Sometime later my parents decided to move the family to Arizona.

A scouting trip was planned in the fall of second grade. The White Sox lost the World Series to the Dodgers in six games, and we were gone, down 55th Street to Archer to Harlem; there we stopped for gas at a Standard Oil station built in a flourish of red, white, and blue details. From the corner of Archer and Harlem it was another two miles to Route 66.

What an adventure! I thought—a three-week vacation during the school year. Not that it would be all fun. My father had rigged a desk for the back seat—a piece of Formica he cut to fit on my lap—so Betty could help me study. Barbara was considered old enough, a high school senior, to stay home.

Of the cities Bobby Troupe mentioned in his song, Amarillo sticks out most in my memory, for the rats my parents said they saw. Even before we reached the Texas Panhandle, the trip had lost most of its appeal for me. Yet another boy was made unhappy by the colors he glimpsed from the back seat of a car.

I did not warm to the brown of rangeland and desert or cactuses shaded a fool's green, prickly to the touch. I was also too young to appreciate earth tones and to know why slender wooden crosses dotted the roadside. They stood singly or in clusters, shafts of somber white against earth and sky.

We exited Route 66 in New Mexico. One day our travel stopped before dark at a motel not far from Alamogordo. I played on a swing set in the late afternoon sun; the pink of dusk was no match for the relentlessly brown surroundings. My father said something about an atomic bomb. From what I could see, we were already there.

With its ranch homes and shopping centers, Phoenix already sprawled in a way unlike Chicago. We stayed with relatives of my Aunt Irene, who was married to my father's brother Harry; yet this family act of kindness did little to draw the brothers any closer. It is embarrassing to admit how little I can remember of our hosts other than their Chihuahua. In several pictures we sit under the shade of our hosts' palm tree; I imagine it was always a dry heat. My mother posed in one photo wearing a cowboy hat that did not quite go with her necklace and skirt.

I sent a postcard to St. Gall. "Dear Sister and classmates," it reads, "Enjoyed seeing desert and mountains." I exaggerated. Sister Francesca handed back the postcard—all cactus, hill, and sky—on our return. During my absence, Sister had only forty-seven students to teach.

One day we crossed the border into Nogales, where I wore a sombrero and sat on a donkey for a photographer. He followed after us until my father bought his picture. It shows me beneath a large sign of Uncle Sam shaking hands with his Mexican counterpart. *Adios, Amigos* appears next to an oversized bottle of Carta Blanca opposite Uncle Sam. No one wanted to pose alongside some pieces of meat that hung outside a butcher shop. The flies were not especially friendly.

There was one other trip of note, when we drove out into the desert to the Theodore Roosevelt Dam. Arizona had yet to grow dependent on asphalt, so the highways were often bad and the direction signs a secret unto themselves. My father tried one back road after another; instead of crumbs we marked our way with a cloud of dust that trailed overhead. Finally my father asked directions of a man on horseback.

He was watching a group of workers with large bags slung over their shoulders. We had stopped alongside a cotton field. For some reason my mother leaned over to ask if she could have a cotton boll to take with her. The man said he would have to ride back to the ranch for permission. My father did not want to wait. We had time to make up.

The picture of us at the dam shows Lake Roosevelt curving into the distance. A few clouds mar an otherwise perfect sky. My parents did not say if they found the desert Southwest to be in any way beautiful; they forever kept their opinion of Arizona to themselves. Because the doctor said, Go, they ventured to a place where their son might live free of mold. They had no choice in the matter.

We stayed long enough to hear about the legend of the Lost Dutchman's Mine, somewhere in the Superstition Mountains on the outskirts of Phoenix. My father kept repeating the story of a gold mine so close to civilization, so ready to change a person's life. Why not his? If the mountains had let go of but one clue, he would have scaled their sides in search of deliverance.

The plan was to go back to Chicago, pack up the house, and move West. For the short run my father would keep working as a fireman and send money. Then something happened. In the second half of the school year, I was absent only six days. Since I seemed to be out of immediate danger, we did not have to rush. Then my father's mother took ill and died in the fall of 1960; that could not help but delay things. For all of third grade, I was sick a total of seven days. By the time I was promoted to Sister Jerome Marie in Room 214, my parents had changed their minds about the great move. They waited until I reached the age of forty to discuss it.

Of all their secrets, this was the one that upset me most. I had dodged a Sunbelt identity by virtue of a few extra healthy days in second and third grade. Because the mold relented or the wind shifted direction, I was destined to become the biographer of a man voted by scholars the worst big-city mayor in American history. This was all too random for me. I lacked my parents' faith.

There were no parades or parties on our return from Arizona. Instead, life in the bungalow belt went on as before. I dared to dream of all the best toys under our Christmas tree despite whispered rumors of coal to be placed in my stocking; this was a joke my parents played on each of their children at one time or another. Some of the hoped-for presents occupied me throughout the winter. Other people's kites flew again in March, as did our flag two months later on Memorial Day.

For years my father mounted the flag in a holder to the right of the living room windows. Summer was the busiest time, with Memorial Day, Flag Day, the Fourth, and Labor Day. It was a scene worthy of the painter Childe Hassam, lacking only confetti to recall Fifth Avenue. When my father's shoulder went bad, he lowered the mailbox and attached a new flag holder to the front railing. When he could no longer manage the steps free of his walker, he might ask me to do the honors. It all made for a study in life changes, with flag.

My Uncle Art was yet another native son who served his city and flew the flag on holidays. I remember seeing him once driving down

Western Avenue; police riding three-wheeler motorcycles always stood out in traffic. Betty and I jumped and waved from the back seat until he waved back. He honestly enjoyed us, and I in turn had loved him from the time he revealed his true self when I was five.

He and my Auntie Fran were still living in the upstairs apartment at my grandmother's on 54th Street. One day I snuck up the front stairs to open the door into the living room. Hanging from a chair was a holster like the one cowboys wore on TV. My uncle caught sight of me just as I pulled out his service revolver. He took the gun from my hands, told me never to do that again, and let me go without further scolding or a spanking. Had he told them, my parents would have provided me with both, I am certain.

My uncle had a gift for wood, even more so than my father; as a favor he built the cabinets for our kitchen. In his spare time he made jigsaw cutouts to announce special events at his house: Disney figures for birthdays, witches at Halloween. On Sundays he would stop working to sit by himself and watch *Victory at Sea*. The television came equipped with a headset that hushed all fighting. My uncle bent forward slightly in his chair as yet another wave of dive bombers rolled across the screen. Only a veteran heard the sounds of fighting.

During World War II he had the distinction of being one of those GIs to serve in both Europe and the Pacific. I can't say for sure when he stood outside our house for his picture, other than that it was winter. The soldier is obviously mugging for the camera. Lifting up his coat a little below the three double rows of brass buttons, he sticks out a foot.

There for all the world to see are his left boot and sock. They are both dry, which means that Arthur Potocki can't possibly be in combat. That as much as anything explains the smile on his face. My uncle was giving thanks, and he knew the right spot to do so, on a walk leading up to the front stairs of a Chicago bungalow. Anyplace else would have seemed unpatriotic.

Love of country on the South Side entailed an exhausting vigilance. We showed the flag at home, on the altar of our new church, and in school classrooms above the chalkboard. If anyone spoke of the Rosenbergs, it was to express support for the verdict in all its finality. This patriotic fervor was meant to wipe away the taint associated with our last names as gangsters, plug-uglies, and union members. The present no less than the past made us suspect.

After Michele and I found a house in 1985, my parents brought us a special housewarming gift. It was a large cotton flag, fairly expensive and hard to find. Barbara told me they did the same for her. Living in a home merely implied loyalty. Flying the flag proved it.

When I taught in college, one history department used a recommended survey text considerably left of my center. The chapter on Eisenhower's America had a picture from the Library of Congress. The caption read, "On July 4, 1961, patriotic residents of a Chicago neighborhood posed in front of their flag-draped homes. Patriotism was a prominent characteristic of the age of consensus." I was three and a half weeks shy of my ninth birthday the day of the picture.

The planning that went into this scene reminded me of Homan Avenue: thirty-nine people lined up from the porch stairs of one house out to the street, thirty-six bungalows, thirty-eight flags, some of them hung from lines running between attic windows and elm trees. Consensus in the bungalow belt required full attention to detail.

The picture first ran in the *Tribune* on July 5, 1961, with the home address of the event's organizer. His wife still lived there, which allowed me to do a follow-up story thirty-seven years later. James "Ed" Cahill was so patriotic, his daughter said, that he regularly changed his route home from work to check and see how businesses displayed their flags. If there was a problem, he stopped and talked to someone, perhaps to advise that the flag should not be displayed in bad weather or after hours without a spotlight on it. Or he might take a flag home to have it washed and sewn. Cahill behaved as my father did. Their veneration was a penance for sins that strangers held against them.

Cahill kept a large scrapbook detailing his preparations for the Fourth. There are letters to newspapers and television stations, with their responses. The plan made its way into gossip columns and onto the back page. Cahill worked on too grand a scale for my father, who was more comfortable sifting through construction debris at the bank across from his firehouse. He took home a discarded statue to clean and paint. Years later I was entrusted with the care of this golden eagle that had once stood sentry alongside a flag pole.

Black Chicagoans are notable by their absence in that picture of the Fourth. The residents of Eddy Street and, for that matter, Homan Avenue did not practice the necessary level of acceptance. Diversity was an idea best left to generations further removed from the grip of Bridgeport. Our parents could but follow and wonder why their children did not.

That is what happened during my freshman year of college, when I qualified to become a "fire cadet." It was a new program intended to give department trainees a taste of the job while freeing veterans from nonessential duties. To my surprise, I passed a somewhat rigorous physical. Running up flights of stairs apparently is yet another trait that can be imprinted on DNA and passed on.

My father spent most of his career stationed at the firehouse on Archer at Sacramento, a fifteen-minute drive from our house. It is a place of red brick and white terra cotta along with flashes of brass and chrome. Echoes of "Hey, Buk-ie Baby" were often heard when somebody wanted to get his attention. Ron Howard used the station for atmosphere in the movie *Backdraft*; my father never knew fires to be so well behaved and slow moving in real life. I was always too afraid to slide down the pole.

My father drove whatever equipment came his way. The greatest challenge may have been that time he spent as a buggy boy, as chauffeurs for department brass were nicknamed. A high-placed son of Hibernia in the same vehicle with a South Side Joey formed a volatile mix that, thankfully, did not ignite. It was at the firehouse that my father also developed his talents as a cook. He often made the meals for his "club," a group of men on the same shift who bought food together. The numbers of old engine companies helped to fill out the lottery tickets he bought sometimes in retirement.

My father kept work largely to himself, even when I was a fifth-grader caught setting fire to a neighbor's garbage can. He never told of carrying out the lifeless body of a three-year-old who reminded him so of his little girl Barbara. This was a story left for my mother to repeat.

We usually called him at the firehouse between 9:30 and 10 every work night. When I asked about his day, there was little beyond a short litany of regular duties, drill, and responding to calls. Sometimes the person who answered the phone would say his truck had been called out, or my father would have to hang up when the alarm rang. In the seconds it took for him to set down the receiver, I could hear the rush of men to their equipment as the siren started. My mother must have heard it too.

I did not have to follow him into the department. All he wanted was for me to make some money and help pay for college. But I rejected out of principle what to him had to seem like a gift from God. Only someone serious about becoming a fireman should be a cadet, and I wasn't serious. Virtue came easy to me then. Sloppy work and a smart mouth always provoked my father's temper. Blows more personal, such as this one, he met with silence.

It was the same when officers took a dislike to him. My father could never make himself polish brass in its human form. Refusing to laugh at a joke or be a good Polack and do as he was told carried a considerable price. He would be rotated out of his company for a month to the least desirable of all assignments, some station in a black neighborhood. This often happened when I was in college.

Exile had one consolation, for me: I got the car. My father did not want anything to happen to the new Galaxie. He drove the car to work for me to pick up after class at De Paul, while it was still daylight. No one talked to me on the El or the street those few blocks from the stop. I was a stranger making his way to a symbol of occupation. And my father was an occupier with few friends. The other men resented a newcomer whose presence confirmed their own lowly status. He suffered his punishment with the same silence that greeted him each morning.

*B*y the second half of my sophomore year, the car came in handy. I had quit my job as a drugstore stock boy in another small act of rebellion. My new job was at a day-care center on North Halsted Street. Two blocks down was the People's Park, where some neighborhood radicals had erected a few pieces of gym equipment to show solidarity with the masses. An outpost of the Industrial Workers of the World sat across from the center. The Wobblies were now-weary revolutionaries with little interest in making converts, unlike the young Satanists and Hare Krishnas who prowled Webster Avenue. Black capes clashed with white robes over the disposition of a soul such as mine.

The way everyone mixed together at the day-care center, the after-school program could have been modeled on a wartime propaganda film. We enrolled children relocated from Appalachia, Mexico, Mississippi, and points between—the area around Lincoln Park had just begun to gentrify. Regardless of origin, my nine-year-olds mimicked Bruce Lee, sang "Everybody Was Kung Fu Fighting," and snuck around with chako sticks. This interest in martial arts nearly eclipsed the tradition of setting off a cherry bomb in the boys' bathroom.

I did after-school care and summer camp. We played sports, went swimming, explored the forest preserves. Without knowing it, I was both big brother and father at the age of nineteen. Ten or eleven years later I ran across the obituary of a teenager shot dead in some disagreement over a radio. By name, age, and address it could have been one of my charges. I had imagined that my influence gave everyone the push they needed to succeed. No one was supposed to lie in a pool of blood between parked cars, a front tire and hubcap his last glimpse of life.

We were all addressed by our title, as in Mr. Doug or Miss Jan. It was Mr. Bruce who took the picture of me policing the playground; he had just bought a 35-millimeter camera and wanted to see if he could develop his own film. Bruce also made leather goods and volunteered for a crisis hotline. Nearly ten years older than me, he had not yet decided what to do with his life. It was a common affliction along Halsted, and one I fell victim to.

After work on Fridays we might go across the street to Otto's, an outdoor restaurant and beer garden. On one of the walls was a Cinemascope-sized mural of the *Tommy* album cover. Armin from my group lived in an upstairs apartment. Mr. Doug, he waved from the back stairs. Bruce advised against getting involved with one of the mothers, who had called me at home on Easter; either my mother or father answered the phone. If I had the car that night, there was a good chance of a date and making out. On Sunday, I would have taken my grandmother to church.

We shared space in the gym with a neighborhood sports program for teens. They mostly walked in from nearby Waller High School, where the melting pot had cooled into racial cliques. Hard fouls under the basket always carried a threat of violence.

The gym was turned into a roller rink Fridays at 6 P.M., when after-school ended. The good tough kids were hired to keep the peace among everyone else. There was one chaperone, Russell, a sophomore maybe. He wore purple work pants and spoke with the cadence of Kentucky or Tennessee; his cheeks were flush with the impatience of a boy wanting to shave. He played point guard, all Converse high-tops and a stutter step that put him on tiptoes.

On Fridays Russell showed off for any girls who might be watching. He would run through his moves—skating backward, balancing on one leg, stopping fast to land again on tiptoes. In the movies someone from Roller Derby would have stepped out of the crowd to reward this display of talent with a contract. But there were no scouts, and the gym closed at eight. Outside, the future waited for Russell next to a punch press somewhere, if he was lucky.

I stayed at the center through the summer of my college graduation. My plan, come fall, was to focus solely on law school. Dropping out after a semester, I had to look for work, which my resumés failed to locate. I also tried to get a job driving a cab but couldn't pass the vision test. Whenever the clerk asked which way the arrow pointed, I misunderstood and gave the opposite answer. He never detected a pattern. Next.

My father still had his hobby job at Wesco Spring, driving when he wasn't translating for the newly hired Polish help. This time, after he found something for me in a wire warehouse on the Near Northwest Side, my finances did not encourage a stand on principle. Rebellion slowly yielded to wisdom.

I scraped up enough money for work shoes. The challenge was to survive the first two weeks, after which I earned a bonus: my employers picked up the cost of the shoes. It was not uncommon for a new hire to leave before that, the way Nick did to work security at the Art Institute. I never saw him there but did read about his adventures in the paper. He was arrested for walking off with some paintings.

Industrial Steel and Wire did business in an old dairy plant without the hint of a tower; making the help feel like serfs would have required too much effort. Bud, my foreman, showed me how to pick orders for coils of brass, copper, phosphor bronze, steel, and whatever. I never bothered to find out what the wire was used for, other than making springs. My lessons on the forklift took place in a residential alley behind the warehouse. That was where I poked a blade through someone's garage door. Bud often took pity on his newest assistant by having me do soda runs to a corner store nearby. In summer we baked under a flat tarred roof while the radio played country and western or the Eagles.

Anyone who masters a forklift deserves better than the label "semi-skilled." It is a nasty little machine with a high center of gravity, eager to tip over on sharp turns. Only by the grace of narrow aisles did I remain upright. None of the company's forklifts had roll bars, but all were equipped with a stick shift. Thus did I join my sisters in figuring out how not to grind gears. The actual forks came in pairs, each one measuring about three feet and weighing forty pounds. These L-shaped pieces made a sharp noise when tossed, which was always a sure sign of boredom on the loading dock.

Our forklifts moved heavy drums and coils. Loading, we angled the forks down to ground level to get under a drum. Forks not touching the floor might pierce the drum's side, and forks at too steep an angle knocked drums over. When containers arrived from overseas, the drums typically were stacked to the roof. This meant lifting the uppermost drums from their top between inverted forks without punching a hole through the roof of the container. We also had to be ready for the occasional surprise of a barrel ripping open from its bottom.

Some of the coils we handled were six feet or more in diameter. The danger here was a loop of half-inch-thick oil-tempered wire getting hung up on the fork. If the coil bands broke, there was an explosion of wire no one wanted to be around. Yet none of our survival skills counted in the way that employers or economists measure the value of a job. Years later I wanted to write a Labor Day newspaper feature, not so much on Industrial Steel as about the people who worked there, several of whom remained from my time. The company said no, publicity might draw the attention of a union organizer. Such concern over pay was uncommon.

Industrial Steel was a regular stop for my father and an opportunity for me to show off my dock skills. I wanted him to see me crack barrels, a tip-and-roll maneuver that required fast feet and hands in a tight spot; mistakes were registered by the crushed toe or finger. This assumed that Charlie had left the premises. He handled most of the dock work and loved his forklift dearly.

Charlie could not read packing slips or labels on the bottles he drank from. The daily ritual of a shot and a beer, commencing at mid-morning, colored Charlie's disposition as well as his face. Drunk or sober, he insisted on calling me Dud. Sometimes we drove together to a warehouse that sold distressed wire at cut rates. Our job was to remove tangles, brush off the rust, and have the coils ready for pickup by our driver. Charlie would speed down side streets in his Impala. The sight of a subcompact drove him to distraction. "Jeez, Dud," he'd shout at me, "how the hell are you supposed to drive a peanut wagon like that?" A few Boilermakers rendered the offending Chevette into a "shitbox."

Charlie cared little for retirement. He was estranged from his family and had but two passions, drink and work. We were accustomed to the one periodically interfering with the other. Since binges usually kept him away till noon, no one thought to worry that day in spring. After work somebody did go over to check on him in the room he rented behind a corner tavern on Drake Avenue. Charlie had died in his sleep. In all the time I knew him, he wore only grey work shirt and pants, black boots, and a blue watch cap. At the wake he didn't look like himself, all dressed in his Sunday best.

Per my father's instructions, I kept secret my college degree and plans to enter graduate school. It was enough to admit to living at home. For the spring and summer of 1975 I simply belonged to the working class. One of my first jobs was to cut wire a few hundredths of an inch in diameter and wire as thick as a finger. The bigger diameters tended to recoil when cut. Sharp ends easily cut through flesh.

Work was, as they say, a revelation, where the time clock ruled in place of a stopwatch. I climbed racks and toted fifty-pound coils, one on each shoulder; my foreman could do two. I discovered the function of steel-tipped work shoes and now refuse to accept them as a fashion statement. When the company bought a second, much larger warehouse a few blocks away, the idea was to make me foreman of the old dairy plant. At that point I revealed my school plans, yet they kept me on anyway. Good help was hard to come by.

At the new warehouse I sprayed weed killer along outside walls and kept a respectful distance from a machine that coated wire with cadmium. When trucks backed into the dock, I pulled a handle to release an articulated diamond-plate platform that extended into the trailer. This allowed our forklifts inside. The trick was to pull the release, jump up, and then land hard on the platform so the lip snapped flat into place. The release spring did not always cooperate, leaving the platform an inverted V too steep to drive over. We all wanted to do it "just like downtown" by setting the platform with one try.

Come winter we huddled in the office—two plywood walls forming a box with two corner brick walls—for its space heater; the cold seemed drawn to wire. In the summer during lunch I climbed onto the roof to sun myself. I did not worry if anyone, least of all commuters on the Milwaukee Road, saw me. My employers let us sunbathe and drink, provided we did it in moderation and kept the inventory free of moisture. Industrial Steel feared only rust and agents of organized labor.

Truck drivers were another source of instruction. They taught me that the best brands of anything were O.P.'s, Other People's; that it was not wise to have girlfriends ride in the cab when a suspicious wife knew the route; and that selective deafness always helped when tying up traffic. From our driver Eddie I learned the art of pacing oneself. Work that had to get done was, and work that could wait did. Eddie was in his late fifties, short, round, and with a crewcut. Like Charlie, he saw no reason ever to stop working. Retirees traveled, but he had done that, been to France in the war, seen the Statue of Liberty on the way home.

My first week I discovered Eddie's gift for language. He had promised to get Bud lunch on the way back from a delivery. It wasn't until after three o'clock that Eddie showed up with the food. "What took so long?" Bud wanted to know. Eddie replied that he had to wait for the condiment he referred to as "cunt juice." Such speech was new to me, which may explain my blushing.

I spent the morning of New Year's Eve 1976 with Eddie in a tavern on North Cicero Avenue. His truck had broken down, and I was sent to pick him up. Under no circumstances could we go back right away. That would have been rushing things unnecessarily. So we sat at the bar. Eddie nursed a drink and treated me to a bowl of chili. In a few hours I would attend a party thrown by the woman who became my wife.

Another regular driver stopped for a delivery or pickup maybe three times a week. He appeared a decent sort, to the point I didn't want him to get in trouble when he forgot his copy of an invoice. After I tracked him down at the Helene Curtis plant on North Avenue, we killed time in his cab as the first shift was let out for the day. People mostly walked home.

His route took him through the West Side, where he complained that black teenagers waited at stoplights to pry open the back door and steal merchandise off his truck. But not this one time, he told me. A group of teens jumped into the trailer only to find it empty. Before they could get out, he accelerated, then came to a sudden stop; bodies were slammed hard against the trailer's front wall. It was a message the driver said he had wanted to send with even more force, though disposal of the bodies might have posed a problem.

I am not above the conceit of a "Blue Like Me" reminiscence, full of working-class bona fides. Then I would be tempted to pass over certain details, like the cum books stacked in the stalls of the men's room so we could pass the time on our breaks, or the men whose wives cheated on them and didn't care they knew, or the liquor that never quite managed to make it all go away. Still, the kind of work my father did for so long avoided the pretense that I later found in most history departments.

On the evening we toured our new building, Bud and I talked before going home. To him expansion signaled ever greater opportunity, a promotion into the office even. This second warehouse stood in a neighborhood of two-flats dating to a little before World War I; the old city fabric wove together work and residence in ways now forgotten. Bud pointed to a row of buildings across the street.

"I just want to own a piece of property before my father dies," he said. No flourish of trumpets followed. Instead we stood together on the sidewalk in the rich twilight of August. That was embellishment enough for any plan nurtured by loading dock and industrial scale.

The noise of work in our new surroundings made me appreciate the quiet that attended closing. Kenny, my other foreman, would yell from the front dock to where I was working with the big coils of oil temper. Each room and corridor stole a bit of sound for itself until Kenny's voice was barely a whisper, five o'clock. All around me stood coils row upon row, lined up against wall and post. Plate-glass windows let in shafts of sunlight—Jesus Light, our daughter calls it—

to show where the particles of dust hovered. In that moment nothing stirred. I hurried out with everyone else before another driver laid on his horn to call us back, and we all went home.

The worst part of work was the commute. You couldn't get there from Homan Avenue directly by expressway. Any of three routes— Kedzie, Pulaski, or Cicero—demanded my full attention to bumper and stoplight for an hour or more. It was the same going home. By the time I parked in front of the house, I just wanted to change and eat. Walking through the gangway failed to register as a significant part of my life.

I don't know of anyone in the neighborhood who took pictures of their gangway. Looking back, we should have, because it was the portal from time clock to dinner table; in my neighborhood, the freedom trail ended in a gangway. Ours was typical, except maybe for the hostas my mother planted, or the grave holding my two frogs that perished on the drive back from Wisconsin, or the music that poured from the open dining room windows on Saturday mornings in warm weather.

Dusting and vacuuming were tasks handed down from my mother to her daughters. Each of the girls played records while they worked. In our house not all music was rock 'n' roll; Elvis ranked behind show tunes and polkas. My sisters moved from living room to dining room washing that man right out of their hair for some enchanted evening, tonight, most of all in the lusty month of May. Only in America, I would say.

"The place remains in my memory as a gray landscape with little vegetation, a clouded sky hovering over dark buildings," wrote William Cronon about Chicago, "and an atmosphere that suddenly made breathing a conscious act." But I suffered an asthma attack in the pristine air at the foot of Pike's Peak, and Cronon missed the back-yards in the city that so frightened him. Dark gangways often yielded to places more congenial, pastoral even, perhaps with an accompanying sound of music. Passing cars go too fast for a good look at what the simple folk do.

Our backyard was both large and lush. I do not say this as someone remembering with a child's eyes. The pictures show it. The yard ran on to forever, or at least to the alley. Because our bungalow went thirty-three years without a garage, my mother had space enough to grow a multitude of flowers. They allowed her another form of self-expression.

There is a picture of me as a two-year-old wanting to climb out of his crib and explore the yard. In the background are some of the flowers that lined our fence with the Dapognys; Mr. Dapogny coordinated the saying of the block rosary sometime in the 1940s. There is also a picture of Betty at age five; she and her doll are posing by the lilac bush. Its color and scent left the yard too soon, before mid-May. Mine was a perennial disappointment, like Chicago baseball.

The ants peeled open our peonies by Memorial Day. Then the white and pink flowers were gone in a week. I had no idea, until Michele explained it to me, that a good garden blooms in sections throughout the summer. My mother knew to endow the yard with a full palette timed to natural rhythms. She practiced her art alone in the same way she did not ask my help to pull weeds.

The irises were planted to mark Betty's spring birth in May 1946. At one time or another our backyard also held lilies, marigolds, zinnias, and mums, along with a snowball bush. The gladiolus all but dripped color, as if a paint brush had been stuck handle-first into the ground. The rose bushes were dusted for bugs though never the lemon tree, a gift from a neighbor two doors up.

The tree was more of a potted bush, growing four feet tall and weighing well over a hundred pounds. It emerged from the basement every May and returned there in late October, under the escort of my father, mostly, and me. The fragrance of lemon blossoms compensated for the thorns that scratched our arms twice a year.

The lemon tree became yet another burden to my parents, like the basement stairs my father had begun to fall down. I postponed the inevitable for a few years by hauling the plant alone. One October they decided to let this memory of my childhood freeze outside, "unless you want it." I did, for the way it blossoms in winter, without regard for basement or calendar.

There is a picture of the yard from the 1940s with my father dressed for work. The still-young fireman is wearing a uniform that consists of double-breasted tunic and slightly oversized hat in the fashion of New York City. But the man standing there is a South Side boy, always true, dressed in his best Scout outfit ever.

To my father's left is a flower bed that ran between the walk and the lawn. The plants disappeared sometime before my birth, unlike the fence, which I recall all too well. It was probably original to the house, wooden posts connected top and bottom with long two-by-fours; attached to this frame was wire fencing scalloped on top. I am not sure which was worse, the wood or the wire. They both were likely to pinch back when touched.

My father could not abide rot and rust; he found enough money to replace the fence in the late spring following our return from Arizona. He worked the long handles of a posthole digger as if they were garden shears. Next he anchored the posts with concrete poured into large oil cans salvaged out of the garbage from behind Blanz's Shell Oil on 55th Street. After lunch he rested on the kitchen floor, his shirt off. I can't get up, he said. I thought it was a joke, not arthritis. At times like this, lying on the floor or couch, he would suddenly refer to himself as Mickey the Mope.

The new fence bordered the yard of neighbors who fled the strife of Englewood. Frank Kissel had retired from one of the railroads, and his sister Minnie Lambert was a widow; Grace was Minnie's adult daughter, also widowed and a parent. Frank stood a little over five and a half feet tall, though muscular into his old age. He typically wore a blue work shirt and dark pants with suspenders. Unless the temperature fell well below freezing, outside he kept to a sweater and Ivy League cap. Frank chewed tobacco, Red Man or Mail Pouch; the juice crusted around the corners of his mouth. Neither Frank nor Minnie showed much interest in dentures.

My father fixed things around their house, and I went to the store for them or shoveled snow. Minnie ventured from the backyard to the front porch and no farther; she favored house dresses with a floral print. Frank took short trips around the neighborhood, to Carl's or the Ace Hardware on Kedzie. By the end of my junior year in college, he could no longer mow the lawn without collapsing.

If he made it far enough to sit against the fence, I went out to ask him how everything was. Fine, he'd say, despite a wheeze in his lungs that did not come from asthma. He refused to see a doctor: No, I just need to rest until I catch my breath. Frank died three months before my graduation. Minnie lasted into the early 1980s. Grace lived mostly alone, except for a large poodle and those few times a year she was remembered as a mother or grandparent. Then she grew too weak to stay on her own and had to be moved out. This was how the block slipped away, one household at a time.

Our yard was big enough for a seesaw and a sandbox, both of which I am sure my father built. In the most technical sense, he did not build the garage, he reassembled it. The homes on our block originally consisted of necessities only. By the logic of 1920s Chicago, a garage verged on decadent luxury. For years my father was content to rent space for his car. He decided on a garage around the time we went to Arizona. My parents probably thought it would make a good selling point.

He paid thirty-five dollars for a two-car bargain on the South Side. Someone had made the mistake of erecting a new garage in the path of the Dan Ryan Expressway, then under construction. The garage was dismantled and delivered to our backyard in sections, to be put back together by my father and a group of men from the firehouse. As a seven-year-old, all I could do was watch, lend my initials to the cement walkway, and wait until the adults stopped work for the day. An unfinished garage invited games of hide-and-seek.

Once it was clear we weren't moving west, my father turned the garage into an extension of the basement. Tools and ladders hung from the walls while lawn furniture went into a crawl space under the rafters. My father also built two small wooden ramps to back the car onto; this gave him just enough room to slide underneath and change the oil. He taught me how to use a grease gun and remove the nut— Don't strip it, Doug, whatever you do—to drain the oil pan. I soon learned that some liquids are best left to cool before handling.

Before we set off on vacation, my father worked on our car in the garage. He hung a light from inside the hood to search out frayed belts and hoses or change spark plugs, usually Champion. We waited until just before leaving to load the trunk. My parents could not bear the thought of a thief breaking into the garage at night to make off with the luggage. After fifth grade I was the only one of the children still going. Both my sisters worked summer jobs.

We ventured beyond the Midwest a second time in June 1964, to celebrate my parents' silver wedding anniversary. For style we drove my Uncle Doc's Pontiac Bonneville convertible, but we should have seen the red leather upholstery as a bad omen. Our skin soon turned the same color. My parents could only afford Fort Lauderdale in the off season. The heat and humidity made everything cheap.

On the way we stopped for gas in Pensacola. Among the comics on a magazine rack in the adjacent restaurant was the August issue of

"All American Men of War," which I have held on to now for over forty years. The cover shows Navajo air ace Johnny Cloud atop a small sheet of ice. His P-51 has just crash-landed into a lake; judging by the two windmills on the shoreline, it must be Holland. Years earlier, a tribal elder had foretold this "watery battle to the death!" Captain Cloud is busy emptying his sidearm at the German plane (Stuka on the cover, Messerschmitt on the inside) bearing down on him. He triumphs by the top half of page fifteen, leaving room at the bottom for a "chewy chewy Tootsie Roll" ad.

Captain Cloud often visited my American history survey class. He helped document the way twelve-year-olds once viewed war: good guys with spirit guides aimed true. I told an engaging story in the classroom, with help from the ads for x-ray specs and the American Body Building Club.

A mostly lighthearted discussion of comic books as a source material for social history would go on for several minutes before I added one final detail about my Pensacola stopover that summer of 1964. There were three restrooms across from the cash register where I paid my twelve cents. Each door had a sign on it, one for Men, another for Women, and a third that read Colored.

We all suffered from sunburn on our trip while I compounded my discomfort by touching a small jellyfish; by comparison the dead alewives that cluttered Rainbow Beach were not so bad, other than for their smell. I took a picture of my father sweating next to a palm tree by a canal somewhere. Our camera could not do justice to the mosquitoes.

The car radio played public service announcements to mark the hundredth anniversary event that day in the War Between the States. Acts of heroism originated from the grey side only. On the way home we drove through Georgia. But the heat followed us north, and it brought along friends. At one motel pool my father could not keep the gnats off his chest where the skin had blistered.

We retreated inside to watch the news. Civil rights workers James Chaney, Andrew Goodman, and Michael Schwerner were reported missing after their release from jail in Philadelphia, Mississippi. FBI agents found their bodies August 4, two days before my mother's fifty-first birthday. It was the same week as the Gulf of Tonkin Incident and a visit to Riverview. Barbara treated me once a summer.

We had a better time at the 1967 world's fair in Montreal. India displayed a motor bike that I dearly wanted and my parents refused to buy. We argued a little, but nothing to keep us from uniting to treat the Soviet pavilion with patriotic care. That year marked the fiftieth anniversary of the October Revolution. A living-history exhibit would have been impressive, if only Stalin had left behind enough old Bolsheviks to staff one. None of us cared for Buckminster Fuller's geodesic dome housing the U.S. exhibit.

I took a picture of my parents sitting in front of the Swiss pavilion. Between them and the entrance are two pieces of very bad modern sculpture, one resembling a huge puddle of cold solder turned upside down and the other an ironworker's doodle painted red. My father looks too exhausted, his hands between his legs, to comment. Sitting alongside him in blue shorts is my mother, always proper, her knees pressed together.

Two years later we went out west again, to Colorado. A leaking radiator made for high adventure in the Rockies and unplanned stops my father must have looked forward to. As a rule he liked to talk with firemen in different towns when we were on vacation. He seemed more relaxed among strangers.

My father drew on Zane Grey novels and episodes of *Gunsmoke* to imagine his West. Fictional terrain is always flatter. We were forced to negotiate real life mountain-road cutbacks and curves in a used Plymouth, although our driver thrilled at the challenge. Without ever forgetting to shift into low, he would yell "Whee!" at the start of a long stretch of downhill highway. My father had been given a few childlike moments to last a lifetime, and he made sure not to waste them.

As Chicagoans we were prairie people unaccustomed to the vertical massings of the West. The landscapes that inspired Ansel Adams rendered us dumb. All we could do was point the Instamatic and shoot. Most everything showed up fuzzy or far away, except for a few snapshots of Mesa Verde. In one my mother is holding on to a safety rail, my father is not.

We all hiked a trail in Rocky Mountain National Park. People from Illinois can never get enough of pine trees and mountain lakes. Back home, "partly cloudy" meant something less striking than a blanket of shadows working its way along the Continental Divide. I didn't so much want to explore the terrain as rip through it. An asthma attack in Colorado Springs left me feeling anxious and angry.

The trail ended considerably above tree line. With my parents nowhere in sight, I had time enough to read. "The very dew seemed to hang upon the trees later into the day than usual, as on the sides of mountains," wrote Thoreau in *Walden*, a work then unknown to me. St. Laurence took care to shield us from notions of life "lived alone, in the woods." The brothers did such a good job that I skipped the nineteenth century entirely for a work more current.

The book is gone now and with it any grass stains to mark the pages from that day. I may have read a section that began, "The reason I became Catholic was that the rule of the institution held that every Sunday each inmate had to attend the church of his choice. I chose the Catholic Church because all the Negroes and Mexicans went there." Or maybe it was, "The white youth of today are coming to see, intuitively, that to escape the onus of the history their fathers made they must face and admit the moral truth concerning the works of their fathers." Presumably that applied to anything done with coils of fire hose.

Heading back down, I passed a hiker maybe three years older. "Good book," he said on seeing my copy of *Soul on Ice*. This college-aged compliment swelled me with pride. I was a fool. My parents hadn't noticed that I brought something along to read.

Five years later I drove to Colorado alone; my father lent me the Galaxie. I returned to the town outside of Rocky Mountain, rented a room, and hiked the trails. I went alone into the mountains and did over thirty miles, if the trail signs were to be trusted. Periodically the sound of an unseen jet echoed across a valley. My hopes of having some kind of vision—by then I was well versed in the Transcendentalists—led to nothing more than a series of vistas I did not then fully appreciate.

Disappointment may explain my forgetting to keep track of the time until well past seven. Ordinarily people don't think of making their way down the side of a mountain after dark without a flashlight. Mine is a sloppy kind of good luck, leading to blisters rather than broken bones and warning citations for "a California rolling stop" in place of jail.

A state trooper did not like my slowing down to stare at him questioning two young hitchhikers. But without jail I could not do as Thoreau had on his release and pick huckleberries, or some Colorado substitute. My father looked surprised to see me home a few days early. We had little choice but to resume our squabble over space in the garage.

He insisted that two full-sized cars would fit. I had to make that happen with an old Impala convertible or submit to being called "a piss-poor driver." It was the same with parallel parking. Anything more than six inches from the curb and he asked, "Are you going to throw out an anchor?" So I learned to caress hubcap to cement without making a scratch. The trick now was to park against one wall of the garage, so long as the chrome trim didn't dig into the studs.

The Impala was an O.P. from Barbara midway through my senior year of college. Before that I mostly depended on the CTA. Buses I understood better than rapid transit. Not until freshman year at De Paul University did I travel to the North Side on my own. I was a greenhorn with instructions and just enough courage to walk down the stairs to the subway on State Street. For three months the meaning of a university A/B stop escaped me, until I figured out why subway signs alternated green with red and why the train today made different stops than the one yesterday.

I never dated girls who lived nearby, and I always wanted the car. Sometimes my night started with sneaking the Galaxie out of the garage, lights off. I was too impressed with myself to bother putting gas back in the tank. This oversight, which happened several times, couldn't have gone unnoticed.

Thirteen years after the garage raising, my father asked some friends to help put a new roof on the house. They stripped off the old shingles with pitchforks before hauling new ones up the ladder on their shoulders. My father was sixty then, and he did not often hang with a young crowd. If anyone said, "Hey, Buke, how 'bout a picture?" he did not tell me to find the camera. My job was to fill a wheelbarrow with debris, nothing more. Insulating the attic took another two years. My father disappeared for hours at a time on Saturdays, alone with his staple gun. I helped carry up rolls of insulation unless my arms broke out in a rash from the fiberglass.

Something drove the men of our neighborhood onto a roof. For years a couple living across the alley from us raised chickens in a coop connected to their garage. No one complained about the smell or the clucking. When the man grew old, it was not his body that failed him. One day his wife walked into the yard and asked me to get him down. He had climbed onto their garage roof.

I went over and said hello. Looking down, he stopped to tell me that he had misplaced something. Why it would be on the roof he didn't say. Maybe you left it in the house, I offered. He considered the possibility for a moment, then climbed down. His wife thanked me before following him inside.

I climbed atop our own garage roof during the winters of 1977 and 1978. They were brutal even by Chicago standards, with a total snowfall of 172 inches. Adding all that snow to the roof threatened a collapse, which my father would have taken personally. So we went out to take turns shoveling from a ladder. The snow blew in my face, under the collar of my coat and down its sleeves; this was the incentive to carve out a spot and stand at an angle on iced-over shingles. We made our way slowly.

Looking up I noticed how my father stopped every few minutes to catch his breath. When a neighbor came out to shovel in the alley, he offered to help, though in fact he mostly watched. I stood on the roof alone, top of the world, beating the old man at his own game. But January is a selfish month, loath to share in victory. Soon enough I stood shivering from the cold and thoughts of mortality. The roof held firm both winters.

If our family stood out from others on the block, it was in the way my parents rejected stereotypes of the dumb, dirty Polack. For some reason they thought real American children should speak only English, and we were not taught Polish. Instead I copied over sloppy homework, learned never again to forge my mother's signature, and found that good grades made adults happy. So did school pants that did not wear out at the knee.

In our house spring cleaning meant precisely that, three months devoted to the eradication of any and all manifestations of dirt. Activity usually peaked on Memorial Day, an orgy of washing, polishing, and dusting. The mattresses were my private little hell. I helped carry them outside and then beat them clean, or vice versa.

Barbara and I were made to honor this tradition long after each of us had moved out. We came each holiday to wash walls and windows;

it was also a way to see how much our parents could still do. By the time he turned eighty-four, my father had given up. He sat on the couch watching some NBA playoff game on television; the number of un-called traveling violations clearly upset him. But that was all toward the end. In the years before, my parents were haunted by the specter of im-migrant fears: let them see you dirty—or obnoxious or unemployed—and you prove them right. This prejudice they felt flourished in the most unexpected places.

"Possibly the South Italians more than any other immigrants rep-resent the pathetic stupidity of agricultural people crowded into city tenements," wrote Jane Addams in *Twenty Years at Hull-House*. By this definition, Homan Avenue was filled with Italians by association, one generation removed from the poverty that followed people across an ocean. Prayers of intercession by the poor were usually addressed to someone like St. Jude. The reformer known as "St. Jane" did not ex-cite that kind of devotion.

One Super Pak shows our house front to back, outside to in. Noth-ing looks to be in any way pathetic or stupid. The backyard pictures probably date from May or June 1952. My mother is quite pregnant. Without ultrasound, she and my father were left to guess the sex of the child. Was she carrying high or low? The picture on the front porch of my father holding his newborn son was from the day of my baptism.

There are two photos showing my godparents, Sis and Charlie. That was how my parents knew them, a sister-in-law and a brother, though I never felt that kind of familiarity. My godmother was preoc-cupied with her husband's drinking while my godfather had left the South Side for a small town downstate. No doubt they meant well.

A photographer at one of the Bridgeport weddings caught Sis and Doc together on the dance floor. Style became them, a bracelet on her forearm, a hankie in his breast pocket. My uncle is holding his wife's hand in his, along with a lit cigar. He possessed an exuberance that lent itself too readily to drink. After their divorce, Sis sometimes remembered my birthday with a card and five dollars enclosed. Even that connection stopped by sixth grade. I have no idea if she or their son is still alive.

For all practical purposes, my Auntie Lou acted as godmother to her nieces and nephews. My mother's older sister never remarried after her husband's death from tuberculosis. There is a Super Pak picture of her, bundled in scarf and coat to withstand the December cold of 1952. Like her sister, my aunt had an eye for fashion; the coat in the picture conceals her love of polka-dot blouses. She was small and quite fond of high heels. With snow or rain, my aunt would fit transparent rubbers over them before going out.

She grouped us by age for our annual trips downtown, usually a movie followed by lunch at the Walnut Room in Marshall Field's. Had the White Sox won the pennant in 1967, she reserved tickets for the two of us to attend a World Series game. She was our guide through the wilderness that existed beyond parish boundaries.

My father enjoyed his sister-in-law, and they often teased each other. This diminished the tension that built in our house on holidays. A roast went in the oven late, or my father wore the same pair of dress pants yet again. Until the very end of his life, my father would announce at Thanksgiving that he wanted "the Pope's nose for Auntie Lou." It was an old Protestant slur that my father and aunt turned into their private joke. Her guilty pleasure was the fatty part of the turkey that covered its posterior.

For some fifty weeks out of the year, my aunt walked the two blocks to Kedzie to catch the bus for her job downtown. The rest of the time she spent on vacation. It was usually by train and always with a group of friends who, like her, were single. There was May with the build of Julia Child and a skill perhaps more important than cooking: May owned a car she drove everywhere. The other friend I recall is

Marie, who worked at the Goldblatt's on 47th and Ashland in Back of the Yards. She wore a noticeably sweet perfume, lilac perhaps, and had hair an iridescent grey.

The sum of my aunt's life, or that part I knew, consists of four images. In one photograph she is standing on the steps of some church or government office, a pair of stone pillars on either side rendering her smaller still. Another two snapshots date from a 1965 vacation in the Blue Ridge Mountains. In one she stands next to a sign for the Pisgah National Forest, and in the other she sits together with three friends on a rock overlooking a mountain valley. I recognize May and Marie.

The last picture is of my grandmother's living room. Five women are seated on the couch beneath a print of "Pinkie" by Thomas Lawrence in the style of Gainsborough. The four women with my aunt I do not remember ever seeing. In this as in all the other pictures and memories I have of her, she is wearing a dress.

My aunt and her friends made choices—about work, men, and living arrangements—the meaning of which scholars now argue. Whatever their interest, none of them will ever see her as I did. She was the aunt who pressed a quarter into my hand at the end of every visit, except the time I mumbled "Is that all?" loud enough for her to hear. Then she gave me more, because a boy my age had expenses to meet. She also lent my sister five thousand dollars to help her husband purchase a podiatry practice. If there is any conclusion to draw from the masculine nickname of Lou, it does not bother me.

My mother chose her brother Charlie as godfather. During the depression he so enjoyed life in the Civilian Conservation Corps that he served two tours, under different names. While stationed in California he encountered a rattlesnake that an alert German shepherd dispatched for him. Charlie returned home with both creatures, the one as a belt and the other for his pet. But the dog did not take to everyone on the South Side. In some kind of fit, it once dragged my grandmother over a fence.

The picture of Charlie with his CCC unit came out of the basement after my father found it all curled up in the corner of a work shelf. The scroll flattened into a 8½-by-25-inch panorama of CCC Camp Castaic, Saugus, California, February 21, 1934. My uncle sits tenth from the right, first row. He is one of 148 men. Of that total, four are black, two wearing cook's aprons. In the background are the scrubby foothills of southern California. They do not appear worthy of much conservation.

My uncle's other tour brought him ninety miles southwest of Chicago to work on the lodge at Starved Rock State Park. That was where he met his wife. My Auntie Dollie looked and often acted like a character out of Steinbeck, generous by nature and without a trace of guile. She also happened to believe that Franklin Roosevelt had plotted to drag the United States into war with Japan; she even dared to express this opinion in the presence of my grandmother. But they did not argue the point while I was around.

My uncle took a job reading meters for the Illinois Power Company. He lived in Utica, which could have been a model for my school reader, *This Is Our Town*. Utica is a small community where St. Mary's Catholic Church sits on a gentle sweep of land. It was here that Jacques Marquette celebrated Mass for God and king before five thousand native people gathered on Holy Thursday, April 11, 1675. My aunt and uncle lived on the south end of town, in a big farmhouse along a dirt road. During visits, my cousin Ray and I headed off for a nearby creek that flowed into the Illinois River. Crawdads watched from a distance in the grass as we tried to catch minnows without falling into the water.

My sisters and I were partial to "the country," as we called it. We liked how the corn swayed, I guess. In my uncle's front yard I could run as hard as I wanted in football or softball and not have to pull up at the curb. If we stayed late, an adult might build a fire and bring out a box of Campfire Marshmallows. We roasted them on sticks.

Barbara spent a Fourth of July there with her cousin Howard when she was twelve. The two of them walked around town in the manner of Tom Sawyer and Becky Thatcher; firecrackers slipped from their fingers with an ease befitting the holiday. My sister now insists on buying fireworks for our daughter every Fourth. She will almost admit to the hope that the right combination of sparklers and Roman candles will land her back in Utica. Jane Addams wrote of being "much gratified when thirty peasant families were induced to move upon the land which they knew so well how to cultivate." We were happy just to visit and work out that urban alienation from nature.

My aunt and uncle had two boys of whom Howard was the older, Barbara's age. For years my mother kept a picture of him under the glass of the dresser in my bedroom; he looked to be no more than eighteen, crew-cut handsome in the fashion of the late fifties. My cousin died in an accident soon after the picture was taken. He was out with friends when the driver lost control of his car. At the time no one would have thought of checking the victims' blood-alcohol level.

We attended a luncheon at the house following Howard's funeral. I remember how dishes of food filled card tables lining either side of the driveway, and how my aunt sat sobbing in a lawn chair. She needed to hear true words of solace, that her son's death had not been in vain, but no one there could say such a thing. Dollie fell into a depression for years. By the time she conquered it, her husband had been diagnosed with Parkinson's. My aunt and uncle are both dead now, buried out of the church atop that gentle sweep of land where Father Marquette once toiled for his lords. The last I heard, Ray had returned from the West Coast to renovate the house.

The Super Pak also has two pictures of my mother sitting on the living room couch with me on her lap. Because the blinds are up, the room is all light and shadow. As children now middle-aged, my sisters and I managed to escape the taint of red eye. Our pictures, in black and white, are the better for it.

Each of us was posed in a swan glider that I remember from the attic. Unlike the wicker bassinet, the glider was purged years ago. My father may have built it in the basement, along with the table and chair in the picture of Betty's first birthday; even the cake had a very good chance of being homemade. But I can't say for sure, or explain all the pictures taken indoors with natural light.

Together my parents possessed the talents of a naif artist. Growing up I found bits and pieces of Kodak relegated to hooks on the pantry pegboard. There was a Brownie box camera with a large viewfinder on top and a "folding" camera where the lens telescoped out. These were like the golf clubs left in a corner of the garage. They belonged to an Edwin and Mary Ann who existed more as a couple than as parents.

I imagine that my mother excelled at composition. Life to her meant a series of ensembles—clothes, pictures, meals, it was all the same. With my father the camera offered yet another mechanical process for him to master. Light meters and shutter speeds provided a new way to take a measure of the man.

In their later years my parents attended Daley Community College to study German; they were about to travel abroad. But they never said anything about photography classes to help them learn an art or hobby. Cameras had a use beyond aesthetics.

Jane Addams wanted a labor museum for immigrants to keep alive the old ways, to be forever quaintly dressed while spinning yarn or sewing. Except that members of the working class, my parents included, were more interested in the future. This is why they took so many photos of their three children early on. We had toys and a yard. The once-poor and too-meek had inherited a house in the bungalow belt. So they made a record on film of a near beatitude coming to pass. Then something better happened along in the form of money.

By the late 1960s the elder Daley was paying city workers not to embarrass him with the kind of strikes that plagued John Lindsay in New York. Then my mother started working, and all the extra trips to Talman provided greater peace of mind than pictures could. At home the camera was relegated to those few minutes between blowing out candles and cutting cake or clearing away the wrapping paper.

As my parents turned their attention to Ford and Kenmore, I grew interested in photography. It was a rite of passage between us. Starting in my mid-twenties I took pictures of old factories and shot industrial panoramas from the top of overpasses. Suddenly an empty storefront with CHIROPODIST spelled out in gilt lettering on plate glass mattered to me very much.

So did the Western Electric Hawthorne plant, where telephones were made and disciples of Frederick Winslow Taylor chased after the help with stopwatches. I shot rolls of film—up close, in the alley, down the street—showing the factory tower outlined in Christmas lights. But the old places affected me too much, and Hawthorne was torn down for a strip mall.

A little before my oral exams, I hounded my friend Bob to come with me out to the West Side. Together we trudged through the snow to an abandoned factory. The Rome of our fathers lay sacked and crumbling. Brick thieves were in the process of stripping away sections of wall; someone else had already carted off the machinery. The real wealth, measured by payroll, was taken long ago. I mostly stopped taking factory pictures soon after.

The Super Pak detailing my arrival from the hospital dates to 1952, which was still prime time for the family camera. There are the parents, sitting on the ottoman with a newborn between them. My father is leaning over, his nose in his wife's hair. They are both smiling. Behind us is the fireplace and mantel my father took out a few years later. He recycled one set of flanking bookshelves into a cabinet. We have it now in Clare's bedroom.

The delivery went without incident, other than that I weighed in excess of nine pounds. Finding a name did not go so easy. My mother had decided on Gregory, for Gregory Peck. But when the nurse asked for a name to record on the birth certificate, she forgot which actor it was to be. In a moment of panic, my mother chose the name of someone else then much in the news. That was how I came to be named for a general and war hero.

There are pictures of relatives meeting the new baby. My Grandma and Grandpa Gurke visited, along with my Uncle Doc. Seated together are my aunts—Sis, Fran, and Lou; a quart of beer rests on the coffee table between them. Plastic slip covers shine in the light. The ottoman, table, and fan chairs from that evening now belong to me.

Next to my grandparents in the dining room is our first television set. The picture tube rested above the speaker in a cherry cabinet on wheels. The TV was moved into my bedroom when asthma kept me home for so much of first grade. I had time enough to become an expert on Flash Gordon and Errol Flynn movies. The carpeting in the front rooms was a muted pink, with a pattern I swear bore an outline of the Korean peninsula.

In one picture my mother has hiked her skirt to above the knee, a bold move with her parents sitting across the room. She probably felt the need on account of Sis. My aunt was an attractive woman with nice legs. That night at our house she wore heels with wraparound straps that tied above the ankle. My mother would not have let any such provocation go unchallenged.

I look at all the pictures from this time with a mix of wonder and memory. I never knew the kitchen had linoleum or that one wall in each of the front rooms was wallpapered; the floral pattern is both large and a little garish. I remember a crack in the base of the torchère that stood next to the other large chair, upholstered in a lime green fabric that was smooth to the touch.

Relatives also visited for the holidays. Judging by the food everyone ate, our assimilation into the mainstream of American culture seems to have stalled outside the kitchen door. Ham was the holiday meat of choice, with side dishes of candied sweet potatoes, Polish sausage, and sauerkraut; whenever my mother opened a can of sauerkraut, she drained the juice into a glass for my father to drink. Children knew to avoid the jar of horseradish. Our favorite meal was beef tongue in a caramelized mushroom gravy; eating another creature's taste buds never struck me as odd. The recipe belonged to Elizabeth, which is to say it was not easy or served often.

My mother liked to watch the *Creative Cookery* television show starring local chefs Antoinette and François Pope. The Popes operated a School of Fancy Cookery somewhere on Michigan Avenue. Their program only whetted my mother's appetite for recipes, which she tore out of the newspaper to stick into drawers and cookbooks or in the space between her mattress and bed frame. Those recipes were culled each year when the mattresses went outside on Memorial Day. My mother was content to lose some of her collection, hold on to a portion, and make hardly any of it. She was always afraid of getting fat.

With his childhood spent in and around a bakery, my father did not treat the kitchen as a woman's place. Both my parents cooked and together made their own sausage. They mixed the ground meat with spices, then hand-cranked the ingredients into pig casings. If the casings ran out, I went to Carl's for more; they were packed in salt that burned to the touch. When Louise moved in with us, she brought along the stub of a cow's horn. Sometimes my parents fit a casing over the horn and stuffed the sausage by thumb.

Our dinners are all a jumble to me now. I would help with the table leaves or polish the good silverware. My Auntie Fran and Uncle Art were our most frequent guests, along with their three girls. Different people sat around the table each decade. Poland mixed with the South Side mixed with spouses from the third generation who heard stories about *Buscia* Elizabeth. For a few years at Easter my parents were able to enjoy their food in the presence of a grandchild. They could never buy enough chocolate to fill her basket. Christ was risen, and Clare had a stomachache.

My mother used a lace tablecloth for the dining room, her attempt at everyday fancy. One evening toward the end of second grade, I spilled a glass of grape soda on the table. The floor squeaked as I rushed in and out of the kitchen for a sponge and towel. Because noise was a distraction from work, my father came up from the basement.

He might have accepted a lie, as when I denied dropping his after-shave into the toilet. But the purple stain discouraged quick-witted sin, and he slapped me across the face. Later that night he walked into the dark of my room; I pretended to be asleep. He bent over and arranged the covers. It was the only time my father ever hit me.

In our house each table carried a different set of rules. My sisters and I knew the dining room was for eating only. We were not invited to join in adult conversation. Talking was for the kitchen. There we were free to express ourselves, provided we could defend an opinion when challenged.

My father gathered information from the four newspapers he read nearly every day. Two were delivered to the house, and the others he picked up at Wesco or the firehouse. We subscribed to the *American* and the *Tribune*, which was an odd pairing. The *American* carried the views of William Randolph Hearst to Chicago, until the *Tribune* took it over in the 1950s. The paper mixed Hollywood cheesecake and po-litical reaction, with a talented group of local sportswriters.

What else is there to say about the *Tribune?* Colonel McCormick wrought it, and the city has never been the same since. I was fascinated by the front-page editorial cartoons, printed in color. They were filled with political characters effeminate, disloyal, corrupt, and Democrat. The drawings brought out my contrary nature to the point that they ruined the GOP for me, both then and now. I am content to wait for a second coming of the New Deal.

We should have had space on the kitchen table for the *Sun-Times*, an amalgam of two anti-*Trib* papers, but it was not to be. Either my father disliked the tabloid format, where the sports pages run backward (not unlike Jimmy Piersall did after hitting his one-hundredth home run), or the comics left something to be desired. After the *American* folded, we took the *Daily News*. That was when my father turned on Mike Royko for some columns critical of the fire department. The bonds that tied in Chicago were not always ethnic.

My father and I began to fight over the news around the time of my eighteenth birthday. In part we fell victim to the times. The world of the counterculture encouraged youth to challenge authority, and I was nothing if not young. We also argued because my father had never been a teenager raised in the security he provided his own children; all notions of adolescent rebellion were foreign to him. The loss of Stanley Bukowski hurt us both.

Protest and the rejection of authority struck my father as the most reckless behavior. He had found what answers he could in life through more or less obedient toil, and he thought it best for everyone else to do the same. People who didn't inevitably drew his scorn. Because I took it upon myself to champion the other side, we argued. I may even have tried to explain why firemen were shot at on the West Side following the death of Martin Luther King.

Our fights continued, if with less frequency, into some of his old age. There was always reason to clash, whether Ronald Reagan, Jesse

Jackson, or one of the Daleys. These disagreements upset him physically. He would grow red in the face, and yelling left him short of breath. At the age of thirty-five I finally took notice.

My mother had the habit of asking, "What do you think?" as if my father and I would calmly share our views on any subject. Much too late in their lives I learned the best answer to her question. During my father's decline I tried to visit in the afternoon, to get them away from the television. We sat in the kitchen and talked. What do you think about President Clinton? I knew to let my father go first, then agree with him or keep quiet. Mark Twain was right: a parent grows wiser the older the child becomes.

No one took pictures in any of the bedrooms. These were considered private places, and so my contortions in pursuit of health went unrecorded. At one point the doctor thought my breathing might improve through an exercise. It consisted of me leaning backward over the edge of the bed until my head touched the floor. This balancing act went on for several minutes, two or three times a week. Presumably what didn't kill me made me stronger.

My mother did what she could for her sick child. The asthma was worst in winter. She fought back with tenderness learned from her own mother, best expressed in words of Polish. It's *ziu-ziu*, she smiled with the arrival of cold weather. We'll take out the *pierzyna* tonight to cover you up, and you'll wear *gacki* in the morning. The feather comforter and long underwear would protect me, or so she prayed. My bedroom underwent incessant vacuuming that she is still able to recall doing.

Stories winning a Newbery or Caldecott Award were out of place on Homan Avenue. Instead my mother read to me in her bedroom from a collection of Golden Books, or we repeated nursery rhymes; blackbirds baked in a pie had to be nice to me, regardless of their number. Someday you'll read all by yourself, she told me. No, I said, that will always be your job. If she was tired, we took a nap together.

Once their closet stopped providing protection, I mostly stayed out of my parents' room, except to find bus fare during college. Petty theft appealed to me more than lectures on money management. Leaving between seven and eight for my early classes was a particular challenge. I knew not to make noise when rummaging for change around the dresser; it would be embarrassing if they woke up. Two quarters got me to the North Side. There were friends at school to borrow money from for the ride home.

My need for independence never extended to an apartment, and my parents never forced the issue. This did not stop me from finding ways to have sex at home or them from hoping I would marry well. We loved one another and lived together as best we could. Once, after a date, I walked in on their making love but managed to keep most of myself hidden in the darkness. For years my mother would tell of the time she saw a disembodied hand late one night. I said nothing to embarrass her.

Probably all the pictures taken in our kitchen were of birthday parties. The composition never varies—cake, guests, yellow wall tiles. But the kitchen also provided my father with his entrance from the basement on a Saturday night. It would have taken a movie camera to capture the full power of a performance.

Of my sisters, Betty was the more attracted to bad boys. They tended to drive cars sporting a window decal of Mr. Horsepower. A cigar-smoking woodpecker, the logo for Clay Smith's Custom Camshafts, promised to improve engine performance in ways I could only imagine. Either by accident or design, my father went downstairs to shower a little before his daughter went out. My guess is that he waited, dripping wet, at the bottom of the stairs for the front doorbell to ring.

A date stepped inside just as the basement door swung open. My father walked into the dining room, a towel barely fitting around his middle. He might say hello or just nod and then stroll into the bathroom. Both my sisters endured this routine, which grew worse for Barbara the day of her wedding. That was when my father gave his future son-in-law a bit of advice: If anything bad happens to my daughter, I'll kill you. The story slipped out during his first hospitalization.

Our kitchen was the brightest room in the house, thanks to the tiles my father installed when I was small. They were the color of scrambled eggs. With the fluorescent ceiling light on, it was hard to fall asleep while studying, though my grandmother did find me on the table that way a few times during college.

The kitchen table is solid wood, dark-stained beech, I think. As a newlywed my mother sat there with her husband, his brothers, and Elizabeth, none of whom spoke much in the morning. This breakfast silence drove my mother to tears, so she did not complain when her mother-in-law moved back to Bridgeport. It was there that Elizabeth saw my father's cousin Ray, returned from the war with a German bride.

Effie probably thought she had married an American. The Skonieczny and the Kropidlowski families let her know otherwise. The only person to take pity on the newlyweds was Elizabeth. It appears my grandmother practiced a selective silence. Perhaps strength was attracted to strength. My grandmother could appreciate a woman left to raise a child after being widowed so young, as this newcomer had been.

Like me, one of Effie and Ray's daughters married someone Jewish. The ground didn't shake and nobody was disowned. I simply brought home a girl from De Paul. She had blue eyes and dark hair along with a common Irish surname. Only in this case, "Harris" traced back to a region both of snakes and Cossacks.

No one knew how my grandmother would react to meeting a Jew. We found out early on, after dinner in the kitchen. Louise led Michele by the hand to her bedroom, where she told stories about the people in her pictures. Then she talked about Poland and her best friend there, who was Jewish. In Radomysl the different religions mixed freely enough, though it was not a safe place after September 1939; the Nazis executed 1,668 Jews a little before Christmas in 1941. As she got ready for bed, my grandmother declared, "You look like a movie star." Over the next six years she never tired of repeating herself.

Our wedding ceremony included a priest and a rabbi as our two families celebrated without incident at a reception where the band played selections from *South Pacific*. My wife and I were to become interpreters of worlds that, for our parents, had been mutually exclusive; my father especially asked questions about the Orthodox and Hasidim while my in-laws learned to distinguish Baptists from Catholics. To me this all constituted proof that anti-Semitism was dead, if it had ever really existed on the South Side. I sometimes tend to dismiss evidence to the contrary, such as the flyer left on our front porch for the 1970 congressional primary. The office address was close to Marquette Park, with the same Hemlock telephone exchange we had.

The man in the picture did not smile. What fanatic does? He warned of the "false doctrine of racial equality" that would ultimately "lead to intermarriage of the races and thus to the destruction of America." We needed "Vidrine on the Washington Scene" to tell the American people, "Communism was started by the Jew Karl Marx." I saved the flyer as a one-of-a-kind artifact, only to get more. They might come on green paper or yellow, warnings about the conspiracy between blacks and Jews. No one ever rang our doorbell to deliver their screed in person.

My dissertation took me to a world that Frederic Thrasher knew well: "Chicago has the character of a vast cultural frontier—a common meeting place for the divergent and antagonistic peoples of the earth." Thrasher found that "Among the most bitter of these intercultural enmities transplanted from the old world is that between the Jews and the Poles." This I wrote about—fights in Douglas Park and an incident of blood libel played out in the summer of 1919. When my book appeared, it was reviewed in a purported newsletter for Polish-American scholars.

The review ran with another that detailed the mistreatment by Jewish families of their Catholic help in Poland between the wars. Whenever such ugliness appears, I want to tell people about my grandmother, that she did not hate like this; neither did my parents or the nuns at St. Gall who taught us to see goodness in others and sinfulness in ourselves. But too many others did hate. The truth first unsettles anyone it would set free.

When her in-laws were not gathered around it (the two Bukowski brothers also moved out), my mother took a degree of comfort from the kitchen table. She was two months pregnant with Barbara at the time of the Japanese attack on Pearl Harbor. If they bombed Chicago, my mother had decided to take cover under the table. When I was six, we used it for a school desk after Sister Amelia delivered her ultimatum—either I learned how to read at home or I repeated first grade because of all my absences.

We worked from an old school reader. I was my mother's second such student; growing up, she had also taught Louise. Again and again my mother read aloud from a page until I memorized the words. The reader was filled with sentences like "Father went to work. Mother went to work, too." Together we fashioned the whole-word method through trial and error. Even now I do not really understand phonics.

It was the same with multiplication. We sat at the table and drilled well past the point that numbers began to dance before my eyes, though hardly ever in the right order. Hearing me struggle, my father must have doubted I would match his seven years of schooling. He grew sarcastic when disappointed. You don't even know four times eight, he shouted from the bathroom before going to bed. Thirty-two, I blurted out. We were both surprised by that answer.

The kitchen chairs, with scroll-cut lyres on the back, could not withstand the pounding of three children and ultimately had to be thrown out. But the table survived for my father to strip and refinish. When my parents bought a new kitchen set, the table went into the basement to wait for the floods. I claimed it before a thunderstorm unleashed enough sewer water to warp the legs.

*T*he back porch was like the gangway—who bothered with pictures? In the summer we ate meals and watched television there. By December it was cold enough for storing soup. The fat formed on top the way ice does over water. If we weren't careful, the bottles of Pepsi froze and exploded in their cartons.

When it was warm my father read the paper on a glider the size of our couch. The cushions rested on a maze of springs, some of which liked to nip at my fingers. I stood in front of the glider one afternoon in May explaining my attempted forgery. "What should we do for punishment?" my father asked. I suggested going without allowance. He knew that a quarter wasn't a terrible sacrifice, but he let it go at that.

A stone step separated the back porch and kitchen. This was my perch, weather permitting. I massed soldiers on the step or drove military vehicles off it. The day of my graduation from De Paul I sat on the step reading a story in the *Tribune* real estate section about managed integration in the neighborhood of Beverly. When people arrived for my party, I tried to show them.

The Christmas tree went on the porch in a bucket until we were ready to decorate. Falling needles and spilled water made a mess of the floor, but it was the holidays so no one cared. Carolers sang on the front porch, my mother baked cookies by the tinful, and surprises had a way of happening. The Christmas Eve I was six, my father worked at the firehouse, but he arranged for a friend to visit.

It was about ten at night and snowing. Santa arrived in his sled pulled by a '55 Chevy. He walked into the living room and stared down at a speechless boy. In order to distill any doubts, he lifted up his suit to show off an ample belly. I could not wait for my father to come home in the morning.

Every box that held our Christmas decorations came with its own story. There had once been a pair of shoes or a blouse, or a pot perhaps, something that gave the right shape to cardboard and, with it, a reprieve from the alley garbage. Big boxes filled with small boxes, and all of them carried the memory of purchases past.

We packed our glass ornaments with great care and added to their number each season. When I married, my parents were relieved to be rid of some. I took globes, single and double, along with triangles, bells, and figures. A snowman and a St. Nicholas are now so old that I hold my breath while handling them. But I lacked the nerve to take the pear with a jack-o'-lantern face.

Our Christmas decorations also carried some political history with them. The oldest ornaments had been made in Europe, from Poland, Czechoslovakia, or Germany. The nativity set was mix-and-match, with several pieces stamped: Germany. It was not "West" or "East" or "German Democratic Republic," though my parents did buy some wooden soldiers with that cold war designation lettered on their bottoms. The shepherds under our tree journeyed either from the Weimar Republic or the new Reich. Like the Wise Men, they fled from a second, more terrible Herod.

The hodgepodge of ornament boxes include several which, if not for the tape holding them together, would now be highly prized collectibles. American Made Glass Tree Ornaments were sold by the United States Mfg. Co. of New York, N.Y.; the box cover features the

Deco design of a tree with ornaments. The Shiny Brite American Made Glass Tree Ornaments were manufactured at two sites in New Jersey and sold by Max Eckhardt and Sons of 45 East 17th Street in New York. The Eckhardts are listed as "Sole Distributors."

Two Shiny Brite boxes have survived the twin scourges of overeager hands and basement floods. One of the lids has a stick tree with ornaments. The other lid shows Uncle Sam shaking hands with Santa Claus. The boxes were holiday exercises in patriotism for my father. He could no more throw away anything with "American" stamped on the top than he would leave the flag out after dark. The box of Glass Christmas-tree Ornaments by the George Franke Sons Co. of Baltimore 1, Maryland, was deemed patriotic by the company it kept, and so was spared.

As other children did, I measured Christmas by the toys under our tree. Quantity did not matter. Somehow my parents always knew what toy would most excite their boy's imagination that year. I still have the sailboat with twenty-inch mast and canvas sails. The idea was for my father to take me to the sailing pond in Hyde Park, but we never found our way there. Other toys, like the Ideal Atomic Cannon, were less than safe. Sitting against the front wall of the living room, I could fire a clothespin the full length of the house. The firearms from Mattel were equally dangerous. My rifle shot a hard plastic bullet capable of taking out a sister's eye.

The train set resulted from a trip downtown to Union Station. Anything that moved on rails fascinated me. With the front door open, I could see straight down the alley to the freight yard on St. Louis Avenue, where the exhaust from diesel engines at work drifted above the wooden fence. If our front porch allowed a glimpse of the railroad's power, television showed the accompanying elements of style. Santa Fe advertised its Super Chief on the 10 O'clock News with Fahey Flynn on Channel 2.

My father took me to Union Station on a Sunday after church. The train shed roof off Canal Street could have been a series of waves frozen in mid-swell; a dusting of snow completed the effect. We went inside to wait on a platform for the Normandy train at Gare Saint-Lazare. The Lionel engine in its grey-and-red "war bonnet" color scheme arrived a few weeks later, and it was quite nice. But the set did not include a platform where a boy could hold his father's hand.

I totally forgot about the American Skyline construction set from Christmas 1962. This was both toy and heresy by Elgo Plastics of Touhy Avenue. Chicago toy manufacturers were supposed to know better than to let boys build Beaux Arts skyscrapers. They mocked the ideal of those glass-and-steel curtains that enshrouded so much of the Loop.

A flood damaged the box, or I lost interest. Either way American Skyline disappeared from my life until one day as an adult I saw it displayed at the Art Institute in an exhibit on construction toys. I contacted the owner, who agreed to sell an extra set. A memory of Christmas Past was made whole again. I even built a skyscraper to pass the time waiting for my infant daughter to fall asleep.

My father needed a tree equal to my toys. His ornaments and tinsel were not intended for ordinary fir branches. If the trees sold on Kedzie Avenue failed to impress him, we took to the car in a quest for the right one. This was determined by degree of size and pine scent; our purchase had to overwhelm on both counts. Only once did he buy a tree from the lot at Tastee Top Ice Cream on Christiana. I helped him carry it home to our back porch. When I could no longer hold up my end, we stopped in the alley for me to catch my breath.

We decorated the tree around the 18th, and gifts were opened Christmas morning. If my father worked at the firehouse Christmas Eve, the children waited until he arrived home, just after 8 A.M. If he had to work Christmas Day, we woke up early so he could watch us.

In college I wanted the gift of rest above all others, since Christmas Eve for me consisted of Midnight Mass and a very late date. The traditional Christmas breakfast did not allow it. My father celebrated the birth of Our Savior in part with a generous helping of fried *kishke*, a sausage made of barley, cow's blood, and ground pork. The aroma was hard to sleep through.

I have two snapshots of my sisters in the living room that Christmas when Betty was nineteen months. In one picture the girls are sitting on a new sled, next to their dollhouse. I vaguely remember it from the attic, very narrow and angled, as if my father had wanted to build the fun house at Riverview in miniature. The other picture shows the entire family, "Dec. 1947" written on the back in pencil. My mother is wearing a dress while my father has on a dark shirt with tie. The four of them look to be a typical suburban family in postwar America. The *kishke* does not give them away.

There are two Super Paks from the Christmas of 1952, when I was five months old. My mother looks beautiful in floral pajamas, holding me on her lap in front of the mantel; hanging above her are three stockings yet to be filled. The picture of Grandma Bukowski sitting with me in front of the tree probably happened a day or two later.

It was one of the few times I seem to have smiled around my grandmother, no doubt thanks in part to the dolls she held in each of her hands. I imagine my father was there, remembering Christmases in Bridgeport. They lacked the trappings of our living room and easy expressions of affection. If a child envies his parent, the reverse must also be true. My father saw how a mother's lap is reserved for special boys.

The Christmas tree in the living room grew smaller as my parents aged. First the live tree yielded to an artificial one; no more did my father have to cut down the trunk so the top could clear the ceiling. When the five-foot imitation fir proved to be a burden, they bought a tree small enough to fit on a table in a corner of the living room. The

Christmas following that miserable Labor Day, my father asked me to help him decorate. I finally saw how serious this task was to him. We had to string the lights just so and place the red tree-apron with the seam to the wall. Baby Jesus went in the center, with the snow-covered ceramic church to His right. My father worked from an ideal which we could not alter lest a part of his world collapse.

The second Christmas he was too unsteady on his feet to help, so I brought Clare along on the assumption he would enjoy seeing her take his place, which he did. The tree stayed up, as was our custom, until the celebration of Three Kings. I started to put the lights away without separating them, but he insisted on coiling each string, the cord wrapped in a tight belt around the middle. He sat at one end of the living room couch, tiny light bulbs piled at his feet. My father still believed that a job done right saved precious time.

He should not have been forced to spend so much of it in the hospital. His final visit, death's onset, coincided with the start of the holiday shopping season the next year. Those twenty days were followed by the prospect of dialysis three times a week. The day after his release I drove over to decorate the tree. I knew to wait until he had returned home.

My father sat on the couch, content to watch me. Periodically he would lean over, elbows resting on knees; his fingers were laced together as if in prayer: Please relieve me of this pain. "I'm fine," he'd say. After I finished, he apologized for not helping more. Those were the last words he spoke to me, along with "I love you" when we said goodbye. He died five days later.

*T*hat the Christmas decorations went downstairs on shelves in the root cellar only increased my regard for the basement. Even the stairs were special, covered with drip-and-speckle-colored tiles that hinted of Jackson Pollock. The sirens always bid me to walk down for the temptations of smell and sound they had arranged. I was partial to turpentine and clothes moaning their way through the washing-machine wringer.

The furnace blew hot air through the house with such force that I still think of heat as something that is both felt and heard. When the weather grew very cold I would play by the vents in the living room for the air to rush against my face. There was also a large grate under the china cabinet in the dining room. My soldiers walked it as a kind of obstacle course. A few unlucky ones fell into the furnace duct work.

The basement sirens tricked me during one of my father's periodic attempts to reconcile with his brother Harry, who still lived close by on 54th Place. I snuck down the stairs to spy on them while they talked by the workbench; for a six-year-old, it was a very clever thing to do. On one of the stairs sat a large bottle I mistook for ginger ale. After swallowing a mouthful, I discovered that vodka tastes entirely different.

I eventually learned enough discipline to be allowed into the basement by myself. It was a place of wonders. My father's workbench alone begs description. The legs are made of angle iron, and the top consists of a wood so hard as to be petrified. The left drawer is for storing the quality rags, either from Roscoe or the Hoekstra Overall Laundry & Supply Company. The right drawer holds electrical equipment, mostly switches and plugs. The vise is bolted onto the left corner of the bench. There are grooves from where hacksaw blades bit into the lead jaws.

The bench has a bottom shelf, about shin high, for holding liquids by the can and gallon. My father insisted on using Carbit Paint, which required a special trip to a store some seven miles away on North Avenue, kitty-corner from Humboldt Park. One gallon survives; it has a drawing of the Rock of Gibraltar on the label along with the words "Permanence" and "Master Painter." I do not remember him ever using any other brand. For that matter I have no memory of the basement without the workbench. Perhaps it came with the house or was a gift from my father's patron saint. Joseph knew the importance of a good bench for doing quality work.

Two large pegboards fill a seven-foot stretch of the wall next to the bench. This is where my father put some of his tools, like the seven putty knives and two wire cutters. Only one pipe wrench is small enough to fit there; the other four hang from the side of the workbench. In a corner between the bench and shower is a set of shelves that go up to the ceiling. This space was reserved for cans filled with nails and for miscellaneous tools, such as his ten files and four chisels, along with three carpenter's aprons. I can see how my uncle's CCC photo sat on a shelf for decades without drawing attention.

To the left, under the pegboards, is an old chest of drawers painted pistachio green. My father used it to store power tools and drop cloths along with scraps of wire that caught his eye. The pipe bender, shaped like a child's crutch, rested between the chest and workbench. He left it with me after we ran conduit for some extra outlets in my basement.

Fourteen large paint brushes hang overhead; another fourteen were given to me. Among them are the largest brushes I have ever seen, as wide as four and a half inches and nearly two inches thick. The bristles are all perfectly clean and as soft as a barber's neck duster. What turpentine failed to remove, gasoline did. I was tempted by either smell.

My father kept a box stuffed with money in the rafters above the washing machine. When he grew too weak, he had me take cash out of it for him, to treat us to dinner or pay for gas to go on a drive. He made me promise the last time in the hospital that I would watch over the box for him. After he died I counted three thousand dollars in fifties and hundreds.

The mess around the workbench is all postmortem. Every tool and accessory had an assigned place—on a shelf or pegboard hook, in a box or drawer; even the coarse rags went into a galvanized garbage can bought for storage. The floor squeegee, with "Chicago Fire Patrol" embossed on the base, doesn't belong inside the shower stall; it should hang from an outside hook. The order of basement things has been broken.

If he were alive my father might explain the need for so many nuts and bolts along with screws, some five thousand in all by my guess. He could never have too much, either of hardware or projects to use it on. There was a system for storing everything in the jars and tiny plastic container drawers, known only unto him.

An old buffet sits at the far end of the basement. This is where my father put the picture of Doc Krops along with a large forty-eight-star flag he could not bring himself to burn. A small drawer held his only diploma, from the Hemphill Diesel Engineering Schools. In June 1937 Hemphill judged Edwin J. Bukowski to be "a competent engineer" of stationary, high-speed, and portable equipment. It was a skill he kept entirely to himself.

Resting on top of the drawers is a now-empty bookcase he built to hold our collection of *National Geographic*. My favorite ones dated to World War II with combat photos and testimonials to "the deep-rooted affection which [B-17 Flying] Fortress crews have for the sturdy ships which bring them back to their bases, time and again, from fierce battles with the enemy forces." I did not think to distinguish between ad copy and truth or ask what a waist-gunner thought as the left wing burst into flames. The magazines were lost in one of those cleaning frenzies that struck downstairs without warning. The copy with its ad from December 1943 escaped by virtue of being in my bedroom at the right time.

My father could spend the better part of a Saturday afternoon in the basement sawing wood while doing two or three loads of wash; there was always a polka playing on the radio, an old Zenith with Bakelite skin. Another of the house sounds I recall is the screen door in the basement slamming shut after he went outside to hang a basketful of clothes. Women's undergarments did not embarrass him, perhaps because he believed the human body was less than beautiful when naked.

The basement was my father's refuge and his prison. Not all his joy in life derived from the workbench, but enough. He could change the tubes in the radio or build shelves or lay down a coat of varnish so smooth the work looked pure downtown. To me it was wizardry of the highest sort. But I was fated to play the impatient apprentice who thought that two pieces of wire attached to a six-volt battery could lift a screwdriver on command. Because the master did not choose to share his secrets, frustration drove me out of the basement, and he stayed there alone.

Eleven empty garment bags hang from the basement rafters. Rather than tell his wife that he loved her, my father bought the bags to protect her clothes from moths. He also built a cement island, ten and a half inches high, with a step, to put the washing machine and dryer beyond reach of the floods. Only he never taught my mother how to use an automatic washer. He did the clothes without complaint.

*P*ictures from the 1930s show my parents to be a very attractive couple. My father looked as impressive in bathing trunks as he did in a double-breasted suit. He was a catch my mother always enjoyed dressing for. And so she smiled, despite her one physical flaw. It has tormented her into old age. "They teased me, 'Mary Ann has horse's teeth, horse's teeth.'" This memory from adolescence I heard for the first time in the emergency room at Holy Cross. She was about to become a hospital patient there for the fourth time in six months.

Around the time my mother turned fifty, she had her teeth pulled for dentures. My Uncle Doc did the work. Not long after, he was forced to end his practice. Something happened during an extraction, and a child bit him. The resulting infection cost him part of a thumb and forefinger. I have a color snapshot from 1965 of my uncle sleeping on our couch. By then he must have taken the job bartending at a country club in a suburb south of the city. He died of cancer in the VA hospital on Damen Avenue a year later. The nurses tied him to his bed for fear that, in delirium, he would try to jump out a window.

My father valued the ability to work more than he ever did his good looks. He dismissed the tyranny of fashion with an observation, "You can't fit stockyard feet in downtown shoes." Or, he might have added, large stomachs in Marshall Field suits. Food was his balm for aching muscles and lungs that filled with smoke; he controlled his weight only when the fire department threatened him with early retirement. My mother did not need any motivation. I can still see her following along with a morning exercise show on television. She always tried to make a friend of sit-ups.

When I grew chubby in fifth grade, she threatened to buy me clothes from Omar the Tentmaker. Betty was given money for keeping her weight down. After our father died, my mother spoke of going on an apple vinegar diet. There was a woman—on Maplewood or Francisco, she couldn't remember which street—who lost a lot of weight that way.

Throughout her life my mother insisted on combining the elements of fashion with faith. She was guided by the need to ask, "Does this match?" and to know that it did. She took the bus downtown to shop until she was eighty. From her I learned to color-coordinate my clothes down to the socks. She will see me sometimes and say, "You look so hond-some," as she did when her husband wore his blue pin-stripe suit. It was the one we buried him in.

My mother always dressed tastefully for downtown and church. She also gave equally to both. After St. Gall stopped Saturday Mass for a lack of English-speaking priests and worshipers, we found her another parish. My mother insisted on putting the St. Gall envelope into the collection; the money would find its way to where it belonged, she thought. Since the C-dif, a rosary often hangs around her neck. The beads are a long-ago gift, she says, from her mother. Everyone else thinks they were sent in the mail not too long ago by a religious order.

My family practiced a philanthropy of modest means. There are no schools or libraries bearing our name, or any need to erase memories of Homestead and Ludlow. My Grandma Gurke gave what she could to Polish missionaries in Africa and my father to a church on one of the Indian reservations out West. They were both people who gave in recognition of their failings. The sums and sins just never amounted to much.

When it was just the two of us at church, my father made a ritual out of preparing for the collection basket. It began during the sermon when he reached into his wallet for some money, whatever he could afford to give that day. The bill was then folded over and over until it became a tiny wad of green paper, like a discarded wrapper of Wrigley's chewing gum. Sinners knew to give their alms without drawing attention.

My mother was different, a Carnegie by inclination if not resources. To her, answering an appeal for money is yet another way of giving glory to God, for which there is no need to apologize or feign humility. Two days do not pass without a solicitation coming to the house. My mother is reluctant to say no. Sometimes we write out checks, other times we pretend to.

My parents shared their faith and their children. I once joked that they argued over everything except the need for disciplining us. Their disagreements were loud and, for me, all too frequent. Shouts of "You son of a bitch" and "To hell with you" were followed by a day's worth of silence between them. Some friends thought my father beat me on a regular basis. This was how he could seem. Yet it was my mother who wielded the strap. My father would rather break off a confrontation than risk hitting anyone.

Their worst fight happened not long after my mother took the job at Ford City. She initially worked a forty-hour week, with as many as three evenings. My father did not like eating supper without her, and he was incensed when she had to work Mother's Day. They fought for a half-hour with an intensity of emotion that kept them from speaking for another three days. Finally my mother promised not to work full time. But she refused to quit her job.

They fought out of ignorance, I think. Despite their life together, my parents did not really understand each other's fears. My father tried to hide his by holding everyone to an impossible standard. Failure was the enemy, and expressions of sympathy would only attract more of the same. Nothing less than full and unrelenting effort counted. In the event of success, he might break into a smile. More often he held off for fear of tempting fate.

My father did not have the time to visit Rainbow Beach on weekdays, and I doubt that he much liked to be around nonswimmers. My mother would take me there on the bus. We joined all those other bathers who did not mind sharing their lakefront with the South Works plant of US Steel. I waded in first, until the water was waist deep; my mother followed in a few minutes, or an hour. Her notion of swimming was to jump up and down a little, then splash water on her chest and arms. Anytime a wave hit us from behind, she gasped as if it were about to carry her away. My mother rarely ventured out more than once an afternoon.

It was strange to see her so vulnerable. If I disliked having to learn to swim (and the doctor said it would be good for my asthma), she was terrified by the thought of drowning. On vacation my father would stand next to her in a pool and try to take her into water over her head. I'll hold you, he'd say, but his wife would have none of it.

In the summer of 1967, after Montreal, we made our annual trip to Wisconsin. A fight the night before made for a quiet drive north. After they made up, my mother decided to go on a fifteen-minute seaplane ride; this time it may have been her husband who was immobilized by fear. So I went, all the time waiting to be sucked out through an open vent. My mother sat in front, delighted to fly over lakes she dared not set foot into. I took the picture that day of her on the dock alongside the pilot in front of his plane. She smiled without prompting.

Five years later, at the age of fifty-nine, my mother took another chance. She decided to start driving. There was even talk she would buy a car to drive to Ford City. But my father made her nervous; he did not take well to the passenger side of the Galaxie. Again I took his place. We studied for her permit and went out together on the streets. Somehow my mother found the courage to pass trucks along Route 83.

She needed just one try to earn her driver's license. It was the only time she ever drove without a relative beside her. Still, my father kept criticizing. He did not know how to provide the encouragement that feeds success. My mother already drove better than his one aunt, who refused ever to shift into reverse, but he expected something more of his wife. Her driving stopped within a year.

The children took the expected sides during their fights. In the end I accepted my father's temper as the unwanted legacy of Bridgeport, made worse by a stroke in 1991. What he said or did mattered less than what he had always kept himself from doing. Around us he practiced the gift of restraint.

My sisters and I argue over people who never stayed the same. Our parents changed from child to child. Barbara had them as the first-born; she was the blessing in a time of war. The family pictures all but resonate in joy and gratitude, showing a princess in her footie pajamas.

There is a snapshot of the three of them in the backyard. My parents are kneeling, shoulder to shoulder. My father holds Barbara up with those two great hands of his. Nothing showed better Why We Fight.

The pictures of Betty are decidedly postwar. They hint at marital strain, the product of colic and bills. Betty absorbed that fatigue to become the most sensitive of the three children. She does not smile for the camera so much as worry. She rarely felt pretty or smart or confident enough to take a good picture.

My sister found it impossible to be the daughter she imagined her mother wanted. The dormitories at the University of Illinois Champaign-Urbana, though chaperoned, still provided too much freedom for a girl fresh from Visitation High School. Betty dropped out at the end of her freshman year. But if one path to a professional life ended, she hoped that an office job downtown might lead to another. My mother assumed that meant the same living arrangement as her sister Lou had. After five, a good girl went home to do family chores. She did not go out on weeknights. A tension developed between my mother and sister that has never quite gone away.

Betty's picture in the St. Gall dedication book foretold the future. My sister had her father's need to serve, and the Girl Scouts offered a place to start. Later she would go to Houston, for her good and that of Shell Oil.

When we talk, the three of us trade in memories of family life. It is considered bad form to bring up fights or punishments. We have reached a kind of understanding, to recall only those times that generated, or should have, a picture. Many of mine date to autumn.

Fall was always my favorite season, that time between the extremes of Chicago heat and cold. My father would rake the leaves into piles and set them on fire along the curb. The flames showed better after dark, the smoke at dusk. I didn't care that burning leaves aggravated my asthma. A little smoke can't hurt, the sirens convinced me.

There is a Friday in November I also remember. My father had come home early from Wesco, so dinner was over in time for a walk. My parents wanted to be back by 6:30, when Don Ameche hosted *International Circus* on Channel 5. *TV Week* says it may have been "'Circus from Italy,' an episode from Varese, Italy, featuring a twirling elephant, a graceful girl who juggles with her feet, a magician who makes a playing radio disappear and a clown's version of 'The Barber of Seville.'" We enjoyed the program nearly as much as Ed Sullivan.

The three of us walked down Homan to 59th Street and back up Christiana. The air was more fall than winter, crisp instead of cold. Every other block I insisted on stopping so we could scan the sky for passing satellites, Soviet or American, but they went too fast or my eyes moved too slow. My parents walked with their arms locked together. Later at home, my father lay in front of the TV, his head resting on two hard foam pillows he had brought back from Arizona. They took on his smell—sweat mostly, with a hint of Old Spice. If he was in the mood, I could lie down next to him and get a bear hug; he would rub my face against his whiskers until I broke loose or cried Uncle. I like to think he obliged me that night.

The exact nature of the attraction between my parents remained a mystery that forced me to accept their relationship on faith. As a believer I could not expect proof of affection, though hints were always welcome. Peasant children beheld miraculous signs while working in the countryside around Lourdes and Fatima. Mine followed indoor labors.

Marriage for me had not meant an end to spring cleaning on Homan Avenue, just a postponement of Memorial Day responsibilities. I proved a dutiful son with a good wife. Together we visited my parents to do their kitchen ceiling and walls a week before our three-month anniversary. The dissolved Spic 'N Span went in one bucket, clean water in the other. I had not forgotten that or how to balance on the extension plank resting on two step ladders. Still, the sponge some-times fell to the floor, and my shoulders ached by the end of the day.

My parents treated us that Friday night in late spring to Chinese food. I sat in a booth remembering the restaurant in earlier days as that pancake house we went to the morning of my graduation from St. Gall, so the question caught me off guard: You want anything to drink? I was unaccustomed to being treated as an adult this way. Then my father broke into song, something playful and romantic from the 1930s; he had never done that in front of me at home. My mother smiled. For her there was never any mystery. They had always loved each other.

Several years later I joined a group interested in saving Comiskey Park from the wrecker's ball. My father had taken me to our first White Sox game there in 1962. I could not imagine the team separate from its ballpark, where a circle of arches always made me think of church, or the breakfast sweet rolls that followed. Catholics comprised the fan base if for no other reason than that, for us, the Black Sox proved beyond all doubt the existence of original sin.

But team owners complained that a ballpark from 1910 with view-obstructing posts stood in the way of profits and had to be razed. Until old age took my parents away, I thought this the greatest loss that had ever befallen me. Then I was made to understand the difference between the absence of person and place.

I wrote a journal of the park's last season. In my desk drawer is a picture from late July 1990 of my wife and parents sitting along the third-base line. On the way to the game that evening, my father re-vealed his secret of breaking curfew in McKinley Park. We had seats just behind the White Sox on-deck circle, close enough that shortstop Ozzie Guillen turned around to see who was yelling at him to tuck in his jersey; it wasn't me. Nine days before, my father had complained to the doctor about headaches that an eight-hour surgery failed to clear up. He never told me about this. I kept the picture because both parents looked so fit.

The book marked the end of my too-long adolescence. Rather, a telephone call on September 10 did. I was mowing the front lawn. Michele did not recognize the voice at the other end of the line. Some woman, she said. My mother could barely get the words out. "Your father says he's going to kill me." A week earlier the doctor had prescribed medication to improve his mood, only to result in this.

The ballpark came down in 1991, the same year as Clare's birth. There would never be three generations of our family sharing a game under those graceful arches. But baseball still managed to bring us together in my parents' backyard four years later. I had just taught Clare how to hit with a bat and wiffle ball. We went over to show them. I pitched while my father caught and called strikes. He staggered with the reflexes of an old man at the approach of each ball.

How his granddaughter did hit that afternoon. He had riled her up by calling everything a strike, even the pitches that bounced in. Stee-rike one, he yelled, raising his right arm in the manner of an umpire; the skin around the biceps had long since begun to sag. Stee-rike two. Clare dug in, waited, and lined my next pitch into the black-eyed Susans. She would not stop hitting for several minutes. Her grandmother cheered from the porch.

It was the only time my father and I ever played ball together. No one thought to look for a camera.

Grandfather and Clare,
November 1991

Grandparents with Clare,
First Communion, 2000

As Father Time

V

DYING

*D*eath tends to come all at once or a little at a time. There are trade-offs either way. A sudden death avoids suffering along with the chance to say goodbye. Yet a slow death often brings pain so intense it demands a person's full attention, to the point that talk becomes a distraction. My father, who was taciturn by nature, took nearly three years to die.

We prayed for him as we now do our mother. Make them better, or take them if their time has come. Those are the choices. That second one has never appealed to me. Faith is tested in all sorts of ways, I suppose.

Before Vatican II the church valued illness and death as tools of instruction. Some of the Corporal and Spiritual Acts of Mercy challenged us to visit the sick, bury the dead, counsel the doubtful, and comfort the sorrowful. I have struggled to do right by the acts for the past thirty years, with mixed results.

The first test did not go especially well. My Auntie Lou had always smoked. This was another of those myriad ways she defined herself. The cost of that decision came due soon after she retired, when the doctors had to remove a lung. It escaped my notice because padding made her appear whole. My aunt pushed fashion in a direction *Vogue* was slow to follow.

She entered the hospital a last time my junior year at De Paul. I managed to visit her once, on Thanksgiving. She lay in a bed at Little Company of Mary, barely conscious. I held her hand and said she would be back home soon. Then I went out on a date. She died a week later.

The once-a-week visits to my grandmother those last months she stayed in a nursing home showed, at best, a marginal improvement on my part. Acts of mercy are easy, if they count at all, when a person feels such serenity with the approach of death. My grandmother would not have thought to impose on anyone, even then. So she sang in what German she remembered and quietly passed away on a cold January day. The ground around the grave site at Resurrection was frozen over by the time her funeral party arrived. A prevailing wind out of the northwest would have carried a trace of cornstarch in the air, either that day or on our return six years later for my Uncle Art.

He had this way of going through cars. First there was the Nash Rambler with the front seats that reclined all the way back, then the blue Plymouth with the fins of a poor man's Cadillac, then whatever the family could afford. He was driving a used car that day a teenager broadsided him at an intersection, and his health was never the same. Around the house we referred to "stomach problems" that attacked his intestines. The doctors used more precise terminology.

Following his stroke in the mid-1980s I made a point of stopping by. I would also take him and my aunt out to eat or for a drive two or three times a year. But I never visited during the three months he was hospitalized with a stomach aneurism. My aunt kept saying he would be home by the end of the week, and I chose to believe her. My Confirmation sponsor died before the hospital could release him.

For years the sense of loss remained gradual, which in turn made it manageable. Death had yet to make a pest of itself. There were pleasant pictures to take at my father's retirement party in 1978 and my wedding two years later; smiles still offered a ready defense against the appearance of old age. As a newlywed I was too preoccupied to do a head count. The photographer did it for me by posing the guests at every table. Doc Krops would not be among them.

After that Barbara and I slowly turned ourselves into paparazzi of the frail. We never would have admitted this, of course. It was just that we wanted something to help remember our parents at this particular birthday or Christmas or Easter. Photographs became our accidental record of physical decline.

More than a year after my father's death, Barbara developed a roll of film that had been left in her camera. We saw pictures of her trip to Italy the previous autumn along with those from Clare's First Communion, fifteen months earlier. The pallor on my father's face frightened me, and it was something I refused to recognize that Sunday afternoon in May when he sat on our living room couch. Five days later I drove him to Holy Cross, where he was diagnosed with congestive heart failure.

My mother, who was close to eighty-six in the photos, looks so much like herself in a smart vest and matching tan slacks. She could still walk the four blocks to the beauty parlor for her standing appointment, Fridays at one. "Jessica hates it when I'm late," she said. Her muddled thoughts worried us only a little then.

My father's health scares increased each year. The blood pressure was something I grew accustomed to, like his headaches. I don't know how he hurt his shoulder or why the decision was made to operate a little after our wedding. Not long after the surgery, his injury became all the rage in baseball, and pitchers were diagnosed with a tear of the rotator cuff.

The doctors wanted him to rehabilitate with weights. He tried for a few weeks before giving up; I was the one who began weight training. My father insisted that work double as therapy. He would drive or hammer his shoulder back to health in the same way he had controlled his weight by putting on a new roof. Eventually he managed to lift his right arm to just above the belt. Anything more required assistance, which he provided himself. Left hand to right wrist in order to extend arm forward: this was the only way he could shake hands, acting as his own puppeteer.

I depended on my parents too much to worry over them. If the Chevette broke down on the North Side, my father pushed it back to Oak Park with his red Ford. When we went on vacation, they gave us their luggage. I repaid them as best I could, with visits and dinner and time set aside to help clean out the gutters or carry Halloween decorations down from the attic. But there were other things that could not be so easily given.

I finished my master's within a span of fourteen months and figured a doctorate would take maybe twice that long. As mistakes go in my life, this was a good one. I dropped out after two years notable only for their lack of progress, and tried to find a job writing. A hundred resumés netted one response, five months before my wedding, to become a cub reporter for a paper in the suburbs. I gladly jumped out of the frying pan.

It never occurred to me to ask why a newspaper contacted someone without a background in journalism. All that mattered was passing the test, a bunch of scrambled facts that I turned into a story about a house fire. Talent carried the day, with an assist from my editor's fondness for drink; liquor gave my efforts a certain gravitas they might otherwise have lacked. I soon learned to invert my pyramids and meet my deadlines for a newspaper that published three times a week. Veteran staffers accepted me, if with something less than a full embrace. I took home $646 a month, paid out in checks that bore such advice as, A Person Is About as Big as the Things That Make Him Angry.

My new career included occasional stabs at the cop beat in Al Capone's old haunt of Cicero. There was no crime there, or so the police insisted. After that, local politics made a nice change of pace. I was fortunate to sit among true believers who heard Congressman Henry Hyde call on them to "stop the Democratic Party from Austin, Texas to Austin Boulevard," which was down the street from the hall where he spoke.

Better yet was my helicopter ride around the army base at Fort McCoy; a group of area politicians had come on a junket. I sat next to one state representative who pointed down to the Wisconsin country-side and shouted, "It looks like delta country," as if dairy cows bore any resemblance to the Viet Cong. The pretext of our visit was to watch the Illinois National Guard on maneuvers. This was during the time of the Muriel Boatlift; a group of detainees found themselves in America's Dairy Land, behind barbed wire. A soldier who pulled guard duty told me she kept a safe distance at night, when some men would masturbate through the fence.

At the time I gave little thought to the feature I did about a nurs-ing home on Pershing Road, beyond priding myself for not writing the puff piece its owners wanted. Still, the smells and the "activity" room filled with wheelchairs bothered me to the point of omitting such facts. I also ignored the plea by one of the residents to get him out. He was sad, I thought without understanding. My father sometimes warned, "Don't get old if you can avoid it." I now know what he meant.

After ten months I left the paper rather than accept an invitation to join the publisher's new cable venture. The glacier that was my educa-tion now moved by fits and starts over an expanse of seven years. I de-fended my dissertation a week before my father's surgery for a brain tumor. He and my mother had gone as long as they could without causing distractions. It was as if they had struck a deal with God, na-ture, or the devil: Let us see Doug accomplish something before we grow too old. They were made to settle for me becoming a doctor of sorts, "entitled to all the rights and honors thereto appertaining," of which there were only a few.

I still have the envelope that came with fifty dollars in it. "Belated Congratulations for Receiving your P.H.D." The handwriting could belong to either one of them. I began teaching at a school the next semester. By then my parents were both seventy-five. They never spoke of this time being "golden" in any way.

*L*eft to themselves, my parents would have worked until their bodies gave out entirely. Because she looked ten to twenty years younger, my mother continued selling clothes into her seventies. Customers instinctively trusted her taste, whether for polyester or cotton. With the employee discount, my mother always managed to find something nice to buy. She carried home a bag with "just a blouse" or a jacket in it so often that I stopped noticing. We found the closets filled with outfits no one ever saw her wear.

Ronald Reagan's embrace of small business could not prevent the women's store in Ford City from going out of business. For a while my mother was left to explore retirement alone. Her husband had his own job, delivering chemicals for a plating supply company. I doubt if he cared that the work might kill him.

My father put in close to forty hours a week making deliveries to places that were either very old or far away. Many of his stops were located a little west of downtown on Lake Street, where loading docks hid under El tracks; he had to guide his truck around the support beams. Other deliveries took him to industrial parks on the fringes of Cook County. Some nights he did not get home before seven.

When we stopped to visit, I saw that he didn't have the strength left to shower and shave or even change out of his work clothes. But my father was happy with a job that returned life to the rhythms he understood. "So I ache a little, it's no big deal," he said. Now it was my turn to worry.

I looked at him and saw the inevitable accident. He would lose control of the truck in bad weather, or the barrel he was rolling onto the dock would tip over and break his leg or cover him in acid. Only it was the owner, a man nearly half my father's age, who died first, of a heart attack. With that the job faded away.

My father did not want the kind of retirement portrayed in the pages of *Modern Maturity*. His wife did, and she soon thrived on a routine centered around the St. Gall seniors' club. Along with regular meetings the club sponsored day trips so members could learn city architecture or the history of the town of Galena: Doug, did you know Ulysses S. Grant once lived there? She rarely missed the parties for Christmas and other special occasions; they did not end until the table centerpieces were raffled off. My mother was competitive that way.

The club consisted mostly of women, and my father's temperament did not allow him to join those few men who belonged. When the seniors sponsored a trip to Las Vegas, both my parents went, but they argued the whole time. Life for my father turned into a routine of odd jobs around the house, driving his wife somewhere, and naps. He slept on the couch a little more each year.

We rented our first house—with my sister Barbara as landlord, or Waclaw—two months before he turned seventy-two. Although neither of my parents thought integration would work in Oak Park, they brought the flag as a housewarming gift anyway. For the next three years I learned what Barbara had gone through. Our house was my father's house, to work on at his pleasure.

He arrived early and unannounced on Saturdays or simply unannounced the rest of the week. Once, while I was away teaching, he came in through the basement window; breaking it provided him the bonus of an extra repair job. Out of irritation I started to do my own work, stripping the woodwork and painting. But I failed to keep him off the decrepit wooden ladder we found in the garage; only he could climb it. During a thunderstorm he had me steady the ladder for him to go up and check for leaking gutters. He stood on the rungs watching the rain run down the roof. After five minutes of this, I told him to come down. Somehow the tone in my voice did not upset him.

Keep your ladder one foot from the wall for every six feet of elevation, he taught me. We switched places after he grew too weak to climb anymore. I would come by the house in late autumn to clean leaves and pine needles out of the gutters, which had to be as clean as the inside of the house. He stood at the foot of the ladder yelling at me while I scooped out leaves into a plastic bag. The rubber soles of my Converse All-Stars were all wrong for the job. You'll slip, he warned from below.

It was during their retirement that my mother made several family albums out of our photographs. An earlier scrapbook spans the period from her courtship to our vacation in the wake of the *Andrea Doria*. That book sat inside a box resting on a shelf in her bedroom closet. Outside of the duplicates, I had never seen any of the photos before. Each page is an exercise in how he and she and they and, finally, we once looked. But there were too many pictures without stories. My father had already died, while my mother found it hard to remember.

Her second compilation covers some twenty-five years and nine volumes, starting in the mid-1960s. The books are filled with the wonderment at how life unfolds, in middle age and beyond. Other people may have taken for granted the images my mother wrapped in protective mylar. But she was a skinny girl from Five Holy Martyrs who was surprised and delighted to have made the acquaintance of travel agents.

My mother wrote down the contents of each scrapbook on a small sheet of yellow paper which she taped to the front cover. "Pictures of Retirement Party / Spain and Portugal / four generations Franny, Grandma Kathy & Brent. / Pictures of the Big Snow Storm." That sheet is centered on a scrapbook cover showing tulips in bloom around a stand of trees. This could be the Black Forest, if such flowers grow there. My parents visited in the late '80s.

"Pictures of Gatlenburgh, / Nathilie and Ernie / San Francisco / Mexico City / Death Valley / Hawaii / First time Las Vegas / Caesars Palace / Douglas College graduation / Grandma's birthday / also Christmas Bill's parents." They visited their old neighbors the Dapognys, attended a bullfight in Mexico, and found a Firemen's Cemetery, in Nevada, I think it was.

My mother showed pictures of "England's visit / Stonehenge" and their trip to Austria, Czechoslovakia, and Poland just after the fall of the Berlin Wall. Bill and my father had to find gasoline for their rented car; Czech was not an easy language for bartering over fuel. When we picked them up at O'Hare, I asked how the trip went. "Thank God she left," my father said of Elizabeth.

The pictures are grouped by associations my mother felt. A bunch of college graduation photos includes a snapshot of me in third grade. A page with four pictures from her fortieth wedding anniversary has just enough space for a black-and-white photo of her mother-in-law. The last page of one book consists entirely of old pictures: my father in the backyard, ca. 1939; that cowboy on his pony at the age of three, with another from second grade; and the three children, when I was maybe six months old. Pictures of family balanced scenes of Pearl Harbor and island gardens.

She never indicated a favorite scrapbook, though it may have been the one with a burnt-orange leather cover. "Pictures of Germany, Austria, / 40th anniversary / Michele baptism / Randy's wedding / Baha Mexico / Cousins Picnic / 70th birthday party Surprise / Various family pictures." Certain pages bear evidence of prayer, both answered and otherwise. My mother prayed for Michele's conversion and for other christenings too.

The doctor would not let her have a fourth child, as she wanted. That son or daughter may have been her best chance for a houseful of grandchildren. Instead my parents were forced to do their grocery shopping alone. If he saw a small child sitting in a cart, my father would say out loud, "I'll take one of those."

He also confided to me that a cousin of his had actually been left in a basket at a relative's doorstep in Bridgeport. He said he would not mind if such a thing happened to him now. It was spoken more as a wish than a secret. Each of his children heard this appeal in one form or another, yet none of us has ever explained our response. We are professionals and polite to a fault. It would be rude of me to inquire why I became the only parent.

My father also left behind a record, though not one of his own making. It showed him over the course of thirteen years, ending three days before his first hospital stay. Reading the notes of those doctor visits, I think of him praying the rosary. He knew his Mysteries, the Joyful and the Glorious, from the Annunciation to the Coronation of Mary. There are also Sorrowful Mysteries. Christ prayed at Gethsemane before He was betrayed and whipped. He was given a crown of thorns and fell three times carrying the cross to Calvary. At three in the afternoon He died. My father endured his own suffering and sorrows. His last words to his wife lying beside him in bed were, "I'm so cold."

He felt no particular connection to the doctors who treated him until my friend Matt opened his practice at 61st and Kedzie. The office stood opposite the Chicago Lawn branch of the public library, where St. Gall students were encouraged to join a summer reading program in fourth and fifth grades. My father liked the idea of going to someone who had once played on his front porch. It also allowed him still another Taylorite efficiency. The Southwest Side City of Chicago senior center was located across the street. He went to the doctor while his wife attended a club meeting.

The worse my father grew, the more he embraced the promise of medicine. In part it stemmed from his affection for Matt. Here was a doctor who talked to him in words he understood and who made house calls. If Matt saw my car parked in front of the house on a Sunday, he stopped in to visit; the doctor was a good son who lived up the street with his widowed mother. Have a drink, my father would say, then another because you can't stand on one leg. He was never too proud to say thanks.

Medicine controlled his pain and prolonged his life, to the point he was tempted to pray to Pfizer before all others. My father was a simple man who wanted to live longer than anyone else. It was a selfishness born of a need to work and to love a wife and grandchild. When he could no longer drive, I took him to see Matt. He would bring an ad ripped out of a magazine and say, "That's what I want." When there was no more to be done, my father saw it as his failure alone. He had done something to make Matt stop caring about him, and he cried.

He often complained about headaches, which had bothered him for decades. Tests revealed a tumor inside his skull. There was an acoustic neuroma, a nonmalignant mass resting on a nerve. My father was told it would continue to grow unless removed. The surgeon sounded optimistic. Conventional surgery would have left my father with little, if any, facial expression. The latest in laser technology promised better results.

In the course of an eight-hour procedure, the surgical team would slice away the tumor; fat from the abdomen would then be used to pack the incision area. There were two unpleasant side effects, the result of routing the laser through an ear passage: the patient lost hearing in that ear and a sense of balance. These problems were presented to my father as manageable. He already suffered from poor hearing on that, his left, side, and a cane would allow him to walk much as before.

After two days in intensive care, he was transferred to a private room. It was a Sunday, and the Bears were on televison. My father lay in bed watching. He had a hole in his head filled with belly fat, a condition that mattered to family and friends only. John Madden did not pass along get-well wishes over the air. That afternoon marked the first time I ever helped anyone onto a toilet.

My father made a fast and, if the surgeon was right, impressive recovery. By finding objects for support, he could walk short distances and avoid using my grandmother's old cane. The doctor was so happy after a year of follow-up visits that he invited his patient to attend a conference, as a prop for a lecture. But hell had not yet frozen over.

I assumed the surgery was a success. "Complains of severe headache, back and leg pain," Matt wrote about a visit the following September. In March 1990 it was "Back aches, lots of headaches." Two months later, "Feels like hell, back hurts." In September, "Still [has] pain, headaches and no sleep." The death threat against his wife followed two days after that.

At one point my father admitted to Michele, rather than to me, that not a day passed without him suffering a headache. But he never would have thought to question the operation itself. The surgeon had done him a favor. Such tumors expand into vital functions of the brain. So my father forced himself to tolerate the persistence of pain. As a good Catholic he might even have offered it up for some special intention. He could then spend most of his free time in prayer and not focus so much on "dry mouth, weakening voice, walks like a drunk." At times he spoke in ways that made it impossible to paraphrase.

There was always a doctor for my father to see. The urologist checked on his prostate while another surgeon looked after his colon. Eventually two ophthalmologists were added to the rotation, one for cataracts and macular degeneration and the other for his corneas. The patient could not keep his blood pressure down around these people.

During 1991 his readings went as high as 200/100, 200/120 and 230/100. Yet in the office of a doctor he once yelled at for making too much noise in the basement, his blood pressure verged on normal. My father's weight, though, concerned us. In early 1992, it was down to 175 pounds at the same time he took six medications daily.

For me the danger now is to reduce my father to his medical file. He was not pain incarnate. He still laughed and complained about the play of his White Sox. For Valentine's Day or their anniversary, he went to the store to buy his wife a card, and they continued to celebrate at special restaurants; neither of them had forgotten how to snuggle. Most of all, he was granted his wish to see a new life come into the family.

Clare was born in late November 1991 at a hospital straddling the border between Oak Park and Chicago. Given the enlightened spirit of the times, I was allowed into the delivery room to see my wife undergo a C-section. If I had asked them, my parents would have gone in my place, such was their excitement. They saw their only grandchild the next day, which was far too long to wait.

Naturally I took a picture. It was not out of fear that death would snatch one or both of them away from me but in the joy that these two lives could meet. I sat my father in the corner of the room closest to Chicago; it seemed only right. For the fourth and perhaps best time, he held an infant in those two powerful hands of his. He suffered a slight stroke eight days later, on Thanksgiving.

Again he recovered quickly and, from what I could tell, totally; he managed to take the Taurus, the last of his new Fords, out of the garage for close to another seven years. I am at heart an optimist, both of convenience and compulsion. Because my father did not complain about his pain, I chose to ignore any signs that would mar the picture of a doting grandparent.

Actually, both my mother and father excelled at the role. When she was two, Clare took a fancy to ring-around-the-rosy. She danced with her grandmother in the living room, and they all fell down. My mother was eighty then. Her husband watched from the couch. The commotion made him smile.

But the manner in which they lavished affection should have given me pause. Their unannounced visits returned, usually on a Sunday night after they had eaten a meal of roast duck at one of the Bohemian restaurants down the street from us. Grandma and Grandpa came without presents, which was unlike them. I had not yet figured out that my father avoided making extra trips in the car whenever possible. "Here's some money. Buy Clare something." And I did, hoping this was no different than the time he had me buy an air conditioner so the baby wouldn't get prickly heat in summer.

My parents were inveterate savers. Aluminum cans, soup labels, box tops—they could not help it. Once Clare began school, she got help for whatever fund-raiser happened along. Her grandparents also opened a mutual fund account in her name. They had put aside enough money from Social Security and a pension that the investment grew to $14,000 after five years and more soon after; the bubble of good times on Wall Street waited for my father's death before bursting. One day it became too hard for him to drive out to the suburbs and see the broker. You should take over the account, he decided.

I finally came to understand that something was passing out of my life when he and Clare first played checkers. He could concentrate for a while, only to grow confused. You're going the wrong way, Grandpa. Losing the game on purpose rather than quitting would have been fine, a grandparent's prerogative. But all he did was sit there and smile, No Mas, and the game had to be called on account of age. I worried about the onset of Alzheimer's.

Or I grasped at signs to the contrary. Just before we moved out of Oak Park, I appeared on a game show in Los Angeles. *Final Jeopardy* went badly because I did not think to ask what dog Boer farmers bred to hunt big game. The only person to know "What is the Rhodesian ridgeback?" was my father. I made a point of telling people that.

When I was first married, my parents might go two weeks without calling. They had work or were on vacation, and I was busy too. This distance bothered me, if short of making an effort to change things. It was enough that we all loved one another, or so I thought.

But the very young no more thrive on absence than do the very old. Toddler and grandparents must share in that first Halloween of pumpkin costume and chocolate. First report cards have to be rewarded with an outpouring of quarters. And we all had to work at the kitchen table to assemble the birdhouse kit when a snow day during junior kindergarten brought us over: Doug, go down and get my drill. Now try to hit the nail, Kiddo.

Unlike other newly minted Ph.D.'s, I did not pursue tenure across state lines. Mine was an unwarranted hope fit for the Children's Crusade, provided it needed someone to teach and write in Chicago, even about Chicago, department heads willing. I had a run of good luck in that regard, six years. When it ended I was free to explore the world of freelance writing, journalism's equivalent of the street snitch. Information, regardless of value, sells cheap in either calling.

I told my parents about the new situation on New Year's Day. They had come down with a virus that lingered the entire month of January; both of them would be too weak to leave the house for the next three weeks. I brought food and unsettling news to start the year 1996. My father probably said to himself yet again that his son was three times seven. In another two years he and my mother would be four times twenty-one, too old for a child so unsettled.

The best reassurance I could offer them was a periodic byline. They did not hear me complain about the long-distance phone bill or how often I had to rewrite a lead or my frustration in having a feature spiked. To them the newspaper carried a kitchen-table cachet that made it appear their son had found a career.

The byline did the same for me, for which I am indebted to the World's Greatest Newspaper. It made possible my calls to such people as Arthur Schlesinger, Jr., and Bob Keeshan. This was how I learned about the politics of history and the history of live children's television in the 1960s. A month before he died, my father said over lunch, "You should have been a journalist." It may be he thought I was. That allowed him to die with one less worry.

The flexibility of my new life made it possible to check in on my parents anytime. Since Barbara and I both lived a half-hour away, distance was never a problem. Instead we worried over a neighborhood now home to a mass of immigrants.

Many of my parents' neighbors had died, and few of the children saw fit to make the bungalows their own. Vacant real estate in Chicago functions much the way a vacuum does in nature; both are filled before long. This change brought my father's life full circle: without moving, he returned to Bridgeport. By default that left me to play the role of Chicago School sociologist.

I saw the garages and back fences reworked to allow pickups into the yard. Flowers are a secondary concern, like the lawn up front; that is for soccer. Where one immigrant group prayed to Our Lady because She appeared at Czestochowa, another reveres Her for Guadalupe. And as the children of May Street joined gangs, so do those on Homan Avenue. Only their choice of weapons and illegal activities differed. In that respect times change.

"Where would we go?" my father countered when we urged him to move. He pretended there were no affordable alternatives to lot 36 / block 5 rather than admit the truth. My father could not envision living anywhere else. He understood home not as some abstraction but as one, and only one, address. So he made friends of the new neighbors to the extent that language allowed, and he used the mechanic down the alley for work on the Taurus. I prevailed on the alderman to write a letter that congratulated Edwin Bukowski on living in the same house for seventy years, and then prayed that no ill would befall its inhabitants.

*T*he cousins' picnic in 1998 took place four weeks and two days before his first hospitalization. One of the Pawlikowskis was taping an oral history. When his turn came, my father needed help walking; his short sleeves exposed bruise marks on both arms from his falls. He talked of Homan Avenue from the perspective that age had granted him. "The Mexicans are doing just what we did," he said. "They want to better themselves." *Banda*, polka, *nortenos*—it was all the same music to him.

Betty skipped that cousins' picnic, as she did all but one of the others. The distance between Chicago and Houston had been growing for years. I remember how excited my father was going there for her wedding. At the age of sixty-five he had another chance for grandchildren; no one ever mentioned Dan's vasectomy. And he wanted to like his new son-in-law, who acted brash in ways we were never allowed to: How ya' doin', Ed? That was part of the appeal for my father.

The ceremony took place in a room off the swimming pool of Betty and Dan's new house, next to a golf course in a suburb with the un-Texas-like name of Humble. Their reception was Sunbelt casual, mostly small talk and drinks. After the guests left, we went to a restaurant for dinner. Seven of us piled into Betty's little Vega, my father squeezed alongside me under the hatchback. He loved this kind of adventure, and how the waiter remembered everyone's order without writing anything down. It was the second day of January 1978, close enough to New Year's for people to dream of the future. My parents did.

They were soon disappointed. Dan was an intense man whose up-bringing in Indiana and Arizona had left him with two, at times antag-onistic, strains of conservatism. My brother-in-law trusted big business over organized labor; believed in rural America as well as the oil depletion allowance; and understood the Second Amendment far better than the First. Chicago made him suspicious, so he carried a handgun in his luggage on visits, just in case. He said "Eye-talian" and dared anyone to correct him.

Dan drank and smoked in the manner of organization men everywhere. My father often remarked, "Your sister is going to be a young widow," and he was right. Michele and I drove down during the 1984 presidential campaign. We all watched the vice-presidential debate between Geraldine Ferraro and the first George Bush. It was pointless to mount a defense of Social Security or political economy that night. I could only watch as our host fell into something ap-proaching apoplexy. Later Rush Limbaugh ministered to him daily as best he could.

A generous early retirement package from Shell Oil allowed Betty and Dan to chase after Zane Grey. My sister and her husband decided they were going to raise cattle. The idea was for them to start off as weekend ranchers. By the logic peculiar to Texas, the commute from Houston to the north central town of Palestine did not constitute in-convenience. Then Dan began complaining of a problem with his toes.

Had he seen a physician right away, it might have made a differ-ence, or at least given Betty peace of mind in the end. The surgeries succeeded only in reducing my brother-in-law to a state of helpless-ness. Betty cared for him throughout. My mother was too sick with stomach flu to attend the funeral, and my father refused to go without her. I stayed to watch over them.

Death did not so much overwhelm our family as change it, or per-haps I should say we accepted the inevitability of such change. Betty had a year to recover. Then she started visiting again, and we returned the favor, the day after Clare graduated kindergarten. The four of us spent a few days in Galveston, saw a ball game in the artifice of the Astrodome, and visited the ranch; Clare liked the burro her aunt kept. At night Clare and I went to sleep while Michele sat with Betty. They talked and sometimes cried together.

We returned home just in time to see my parents before they left for Wisconsin. Barbara and Bill joined us for dinner together at a Mexican restaurant. My father felt sick the next day. That may have been why he saw the doctor. "Upset stomach since yesterday; vomit this AM; w/o fever, chills; feels weak, body pain; sleeps mostly fair." My father was now on eight medications. What, if any, effect they had on his appetite I don't know.

The rest of the summer dragged. For several weeks I tried to interest my father in fixing his glide-assist vacuum. It was the kind of work that should have led him into the basement to take the machine apart. With the door closed, he would be free to talk to himself or address exposed belts and wires; almost always he whistled. Then, if the job looked too complicated, he would take me along on a Saturday to price out repairs: You want a hot dog?

But he was content that July and August to have me handle everything. The one time we went to a shop, all he could do was say, Fine. I wanted him to be his old self, when he would have walked out in disgust and told no one in particular what a dump the place was and yell at me for taking him there.

Days I didn't visit were spent waiting for calls. I tried to avoid phoning my parents because there was no guarantee anyone would answer. By late August, if he was alone, my father couldn't get to the phone. "Yeah, I know you called," he would say, "but I was on the floor at the time." This gallows humor both amused and frightened me.

Matt visited two days after my father's eighty-fifth birthday to find evidence of hypoglycemia along with renal failure. The Thursday before Labor Day I drove him to his doctor's appointment. In order to get down the stairs, I had to lift my father by the back of his pants and his belt. "Doc, you got to mix me up something powerful in a shot," he said when we walked in. "I'm feeling weak."

The notes for that visit read, "Fell 3 times in last 3 days; poor appetite; slight indigestion; mouth dry; back hurting due to fall; w/o dizziness, LOC [loss of consciousness]; feels very weak." He now weighed 146 pounds. Five days later we went to the hospital together. I helped the nurse get him into bed; his body looked all shriveled against the sheets. I assumed that was a sign of impending death and so began planning the eulogy. None of us was prepared for his release after two weeks. He should have died that first time, Barbara has said to me.

All summer Mark McGwire and Sammy Sosa chased the asterisk belonging to Roger Maris. Their race drew the interest of my mother, who betrayed the same affection for Sosa she once had for Hack Wilson. I took my father to Holy Cross for an upper GI test the Saturday before Labor Day. McGwire hit his 60th in an afternoon game. The home run was measured at 380 feet, a trip of maybe five seconds' duration that would have taken my father most of the day to walk.

A few hours after my father was admitted on Tuesday, McGwire set the record. I thought it would be fun to celebrate. Clare followed me into the backyard, and we lit some sparklers left over from the Fourth of July. If one of the patients put the game on, my father could have listened in bed. He preferred Ruth to all the others.

My father was too preoccupied to talk much baseball that September. More than anything he wanted to know what his test results said. Read together, they showed that death was approaching but not imminent; the message hid between columns of numbers and ranges. The diabetes and weak kidneys were our major concern. None of us quite understood how six weeks of home therapy would help, or why elevating the couch with two bricks under each leg mattered. But we did not want our father to die, and so we did as we were told.

Betty arrived on Wednesday for a two-week stay. She joined her sister in a thorough cleaning of the house. Another of the symptoms we had chosen to ignore was the appearance of clutter. Newspapers and aluminum cans collected on the back porch while unopened mail took over the dining room table. My sisters struck back by going after all signs of mess, as if sloppiness bore the diseases of old age.

The bills were always paid on time; this my father roused himself from his death bed to do. It was the solicitations that piled up. A missionary's appeal could not be disposed of without discussion, an activity that drained what little energy my parents had left. For the next few months we screened the mail, and the missions did without.

My father was left with just a few things to wear. Most of his wardrobe had been bought when he still weighed two hundred pounds. People always pack away the clothes of a loved one, and my sisters wanted to be good daughters to the end. They did not know he would live long enough to gain back almost all his weight.

Until that September we had done little to intervene in the lives of our parents. We did not make them move or hire a cleaning service. If they asked, Michele balanced their checking account, but she never presumed to write checks in their name. They also trusted me to draft letters to Medicare for them. Otherwise they wanted to be left alone. The hospital ended all that.

Over the next two months, until our resolve weakened, we attacked everything. The clothes were suspect because the sweat in the fabric carried hints of illness or age, so they had to be purged. My parents often told me they resented this intrusion into their personal effects. There would be others equally unpleasant. My mother's cache of recipes had no chance.

But if this was war, our advance faltered by the onset of winter. As children we had been raised above all else to respect and obey. Thirty years later there was no precedent to draw on that allowed us to take charge and reorder their lives. We had to settle for half-measures: they could still go shopping or to church, but only if one of us drove them. Nobody was satisfied, and yet the alternative of a fully dictated dependence frightened everyone.

Good intentions could not stop a retreat into rooms away from our parents. Betty would volunteer to cook a meal, Texas style, and Barbara would help or make drinks. After a while I went to check on them. My father sat alone on the couch or alongside his wife. Because there was no way to shield them, we hid in shame around the kitchen table. Our parents were slipping away, and we could do nothing to stop it.

My father returned home from the hospital cold and prone to tears. His crying had started in the hospital. There was no identifiable trigger; a conversation stopped the instant my father got, in his words, "all weepy." He grew worse with each hospital stay, and the crying never went away at home. Still, he seemed to get better those twelve weeks following his release.

After a month he had the strength to attend church Saturday afternoons and dinner afterward. When it was my turn, we took them to the Dynasty on Archer Avenue, a place they liked in that time before Labor Day. The waitresses knew them, and my mother enjoyed the free glass of wine with dinner. More often than not, my father gave her his glass to drink as well. They laughed to the point of tears when Clare asked if she could wear high heels to her First Communion next year.

Going to church at St. Gall took up half the afternoon and evening. Still, its familiarity pleased me. The pew was filled again with the parents and children of our family. On some days Michele and I were among the youngest adult worshipers there. The sound of the

Kedzie bus made me think of other, more crowded, afternoons when I went to Confession or Mass. The green glazed walls called forth echoes and, with them, yet other memories.

I always stood behind my father on the way to Communion, in case he stumbled. Such episodes came without warning as the strength went out of his legs. When it happened, we might sit together on the steps outside church to wait until he could walk again. I did my best to keep him from crying.

He never liked what he ordered at the Dynasty—the pork chop was too tough or the ribs too fatty. I learned to disregard such talk. He simply needed to go through the motions, to pretend it was even six months ago. This was all my father wanted, along with an end to his pain and the Sunday *Sun-Times* for its TV guide. But I made too much of a show one night getting the paper, a fancy left-hand turn against traffic on 55th Street by the airport followed by an in-and-out at the convenience store. "Got it" was the wrong thing to say. My father disliked feeling that people had made an effort on his behalf. Two Sunday papers were a waste of money, he decided.

For a few months he could manage the basement stairs and do the wash; that, or it waited for one of the children. We took walks around the block, and he told me how he would start driving again soon. But his balance was never very good. Twice he fell trying to help me do work around the yard. From the ladder I saw him bounce against the fence and fall back-first onto the sidewalk. Before I could get down to help, he pulled himself up by grabbing onto the fence. The other time his body landed across the cellar stairs. Again he struggled to his feet in order to beat the ten-count that sounded in his good ear.

He was now made to submit before others. Someone else would bathe, shave, and toward the end, dress him. But he insisted on doing two of his household chores for as long as his strength allowed. They mattered to him in ways I could only guess at.

Every other month we changed furnace filters and flipped the mattress in his bedroom. He wobbled down the stairs to watch me insert the new filters; I pretended the old ones were dirty. In the bedroom he leaned against the wall as we tossed the mattress, first head to toe and then bottom side up. He said, "Good," followed by "Thanks."

Bill and I began driving him at least once a week to a chiropractor for the pain. If nothing else, the visits took him out of the house for a nice massage. The doctor was a sincere young man with a baby on the way. He feared that immunization shots for childhood diseases did more harm than good. Children needed to build up their resistance through exposure, he said to me. I made an effort to be polite.

It was at the chiropractor that I noticed how much my father's body now rebelled against him. "I'm going as fast as I can," he told anyone waiting for him to pass in the hallway. He said the same whether using the cane or walker. As an extra betrayal, his hands began to ignore his pockets; a wallet might go in but never out. So I took to guiding one hand into a pants pocket so he could have money ready to pay the bill. It was a simple act that kept his pride intact.

Without telling anyone, my father declared himself fit to drive on December 8, a holy day of obligation. In the morning he and my mother drove to St. Gall for Mass to celebrate Mary's conception free of original sin, followed by grocery shopping. The problem started when he tried to park in front of the house. My father kept getting the car hung up on the curb. He had to go find his next-door neighbor. Manuel was good enough to put the car into the garage. My father never drove again.

He kept the Taurus for another year. We said Betty would need something to drive when she visited until my father fell victim to his own logic. It was cheaper to rent a car than pay auto insurance. So my parents decided to give me the Ford; this way it stayed in the family, and they could still ride in it to church. When I called Allstate to cancel the policy, the agent told me it dated from 1943. I tried without much success to get my father excited about the size of the refund. The billy club stayed where he kept it, under the driver's seat. I hung the license plates, still EB 5415, in my garage.

We were lucky. The problem of an elderly parent driving was settled after one harmless incident. The shame attendant to that day kept him from trying again. My father could just as easily have driven the car into a telephone pole or through a store window. These things happen all the time. Several months earlier a seventy-six-year-old woman my mother knew from St. Gall struck thirteen pedestrians while driving downtown. Something went wrong as she exited a parking garage, and three people were left dead.

This accident did not cause me to hide the car keys. Driving defined my father much the way work had; without the ability to do either, he would only die sooner. I simply did not want to become a full-time chauffeur or emasculate one of my parents with a roll of bus tokens. Letting him drive for so long was a gamble with other people's lives. It is a game of ante up and be anted up, your parents or mine.

*B*etween us, Barbara and I visited four times a week; Bill would drop in when he could. Still, my parents always seemed to need help. They were out of toilet paper or one-minute oatmeal, and it couldn't wait. Somebody went to the store for them, only to find that my mother had put the Quaker Oats on the wrong shelf, next to the unopened Charmin. Other crises we could not resolve, and so my father's first thousand-dollar hearing aid disappeared down the toilet and their dog chewed the replacement into a tiny pile of junk. By spring it was obvious we needed to hire a live-in for them. Rather than put our parents in a home, we brought the home to them. If nothing else, my father would be able to stare at walls of his own painting.

We made the decision after he was hospitalized for dementia, the result of impacted bowels. My father did not drink or do enough to be regular. Once the laxatives cleaned him out, he became himself again, and the imaginary visitors disappeared. A minimum of eight glasses of water a day was prescribed to prevent a relapse. He had to forget his complaints over the past eleven years about "urinating frequently" and find the strength necessary to walk to the bathroom. Or he could smell or go crazy again in a few weeks. As in all other health issues, the final decision was left to him.

The new era began with a stretch limousine pulling up in front of the house on a Saturday morning in early April. Five women sent by an agency stepped out to be interviewed. Barbara and Michele asked most of the questions. All five applicants were either Polish or Lithuanian nationals, so those with the worst English skills were eliminated first. Next, anyone who seemed too rigid or unlikely to bond with a sick old man was disqualified. We also wanted somebody who could cook.

More than anything, we looked for that one person who most resembled us. Then it would not seem that we were entrusting our parents to a stranger. By a joint process of elimination and rationalization, we chose Ona, an attractive Lithuanian immigrant in her late forties. If we were not satisfied, the service that brought her offered a one-year guarantee with free replacement.

My father had already accustomed himself to the visiting nurses who were assigned to him after each hospital stay. They came once or twice a week for six weeks. The women were all pleasant, as were my parents. For the first time in their lives, a black person sat in their living room and kitchen. No one brought up Marquette Park or other unpleasantries from 1966.

The caregiver arrangement worked well enough for almost a year and a half. Ona made sure that my father took his pills and everyone had three meals a day. She was in large part responsible for both parents gaining so much weight. Despite my mother's complaints of being fat, we took this as a plus. There were too many skinny old people at church on Saturday.

My mother also thought she had a real friend, someone who would walk with her to the beauty parlor and go shopping at the St. Vincent De Paul store that took the place of Minicino's Certified at 54th and Kedzie. They brought home bargains by the bagful. Such clothes did not exist so cheap back home, where Ona had two teenaged daughters. Overseas postage turned resale into haute couture.

Ona practiced an immigrant's calculus. My parents were her job, and she did it well enough to keep from being fired. She might lose her temper with my mother and mock her for being slow or uncertain on the stairs, but she mostly managed to hide these moments from us. Her great fear was deportation, which she fully intended to avoid.

The health crises abated long enough for Barbara to consider another fishing trip to Wisconsin in June. What if he fell out of the boat? I asked. She thought they could fish from the pier. And if he needed to get to a bathroom fast? My sister found it hard to let go.

Instead we celebrated our parents' sixtieth wedding anniversary with a small party. Betty scheduled her visit to coincide with June 17. The two of us were talking in my living room that afternoon when the phone rang. My mother was all dressed and waiting to go to lunch with her sister Fran, except that Betty had never promised to take them. The difference between wish and fact was beginning to dissolve. Of the two of them, my father looked the stronger that evening at dinner. He wore his good blue suit.

He went off the arthritis medicine in October because it was too hard on his kidneys. A cortisone shot provided some temporary relief. When it wore off, he could do little more than lie or sit on the couch for hours on end. The arthritis in his back dictated when and for how long he could walk. The cane was mostly left in a corner of the hallway. A walker allowed him to move with less pressure on his back. He leaned on it with such force that we had to get a replacement within a year.

Betty came again in late fall. She volunteered for the unpleasant task of preparing power-of-attorney forms for property and health care. Barbara was named the primary "attorney-in-fact," with me to follow and then Betty. Both our parents initialed the section that began "I do not want my life to be prolonged nor do I want life-sustaining treatment" on the morning of November 20, their granddaughter's eighth birthday; my father's signature had not deteriorated nearly as much as my mother's. Betty drove them over for the party that evening.

I opposed the "do not resuscitate" clause without fighting it. To say that my parents were in good health qualified either as lie or delusion. If anything, my father showed an extraordinary capacity for suffering; it was his strength—and curse—to be able to go on this way. And yet I did not want to lose them even as they now were. In the end I did the math of three times seven and hoped they had made the right decision.

Each hospital stay brought another round of home therapy along with nurses' visits. This allowed us to think he would get better and stronger. But his walking grew steadily worse. At Christmas he stepped on my mother's foot so hard she nearly crumpled to the floor in pain. I told you to move, dammit. We all ignored the way he shouted and the tears running down her cheeks. It was the holidays.

I am inclined to treat pharmaceuticals with a skepticism befitting Christian Science or that young chiropractor we visited. This may be why Barbara and I argued so often over our father's pills. To me, eight drugs a day were too many. My sister was trained to think otherwise.

She believed that everything—blood pressure, diabetes, the problems with sleep and depression—was best treated through medication. It might have been the right course if only his condition had remained stable. But he possessed a seemingly infinite capacity for decline. What showed so much promise one week did little if anything the next. We found this out again on Easter Day. My mother was in the hospital for observation after passing out at the kitchen table.

The year before, my father had sat on the couch acting out his delusions from extreme constipation. This second Easter he lay in the living room sound asleep. Ona had put him on the couch before taking the afternoon off. Michele and I got to the house early to prepare dinner; Barbara and Bill arrived a little later. For the past ten years my father had been unable to sleep. Now he did not wake up regardless of how hard I shook him. Maybe it was the smell of Polish sausage that worked.

His mood and sleep medications bothered me the most. They were like dope in the way they slowed down speech and movement. After the first few combinations I was ready to stop giving him these drugs. But as the eldest, Barbara decided we had to keep trying.

After dinner he wanted to talk to his wife in the hospital. I called my mother's room; unlike later visits, she still possessed the strength and coordination to pick up the phone. My father began talking to her before I could put the receiver in his hand; when I did, he saw no reason to start over. My mother came home four days later. All she needed was some beta-blockers.

Everyone sat in the kitchen celebrating. We then decided to move to the living room, where it was sunny. First I shut off the television they were watching. "See what you did," my father scolded her, "now we have no TV." I asked him what he was talking about.

Within seconds I was calling him silly, and he was telling me to leave. To show that he didn't need anyone's help for anything, he got up and started for the bathroom. "I thought you could do it all by yourself," I shouted when he fell in the hallway. He did not want me lifting him up, so I did it to spite him. Then I left.

Michele and Clare sat with me in the car. We were supposed to go to the zoo that afternoon. When the worst of the anger passed, I walked back in without any real desire to apologize. Ona had managed to get him onto the couch, and he had no recollection of arguing. I convinced Barbara to stop the depression medication for a while.

He was lucid during Clare's First Communion that May, and the party provided some relief from our anxieties. Everyone, most of all the grandparents, wanted to be around the beautiful child in her white dress. I kept quiet about how my father had called the day before, crying and asking why Matt wasn't answering his office phone. By Friday we were at Holy Cross, where tests showed he was suffering from congestive heart failure.

It was miserable out, cold with a November-grey sky. We passed the time talking to a woman who had finished having some x-rays taken; she looked to be maybe ten years younger than my father. She put on an old spring coat, too thin for such a day, and went outside to wait at a bus stop. Looking at her, my father said, "That would be me if it weren't for you and Barbara." Later I called my sister to repeat what he said.

There was one perfect day that summer, just after Clare got out of school for vacation. I took her with my parents to the optician's at 95th and Central in the suburb of Oak Lawn; my father had been getting his glasses there for years. I brought my parents into the store one at a time. The glasses were fitted and paid for. I got everyone back in the car just as the rain started.

"I want a hot tamale," my father announced in total disregard of the weather. I stopped at one, then another, a third, and finally a fourth hot dog stand along Pulaski Road. Each time Clare and I ran out, to get soaked in the course of those ten feet from car door to order window. My daughter did not mind because she knew her grandfather would arrange to pay her back with ice cream or a handful of change. The thunderstorm and our quest more or less ended together just north of 55th Street. My father got his tamale, a Tom Tom, with the boy and girl yet conversing on the wrapper.

Not long after, it was time for a haircut. Our neighbor Casey had died well before that final summer. But the loss of a barber did not alter the rules my father lived by, on the job or in retirement. Because fire department regulations called for short hair, he visited the same barber shop on Kedzie Avenue I went to as a boy. I drove him every six to eight weeks. In spring my father made sure to ask Sam about the state of his tomato plants. They sat in the front window until the weather turned warm enough for planting.

We had to wait an extra month, until August, even though the sign in the window said Sam would be back from vacation in July. When we arrived the shop was filled with men, mostly retired, asking Sam about the delay. "My sister-in-law had a fever and couldn't fly," he tried to explain. But he couldn't get them to understand.

"Sam," asked a customer with pants that reached up over his stomach to his ribs, "where did you go?" Finally, out of frustration, Sam cracked, "To Sicily to see the Pope and his wife." The men who were able to hear laughed at this joke and another: "To see the Pope? Did you give him an envelope? Did you give him a boost?"

"Yeah," Sam answered, his back to a mirror lined on one side with holy cards of the Blessed Virgin, "I gave the Pope a boost."

One of the men knew Sam from Taylor Street, from before the elder Daley swept away the old places for his university. "Cut all the hair, Sam," he instructed. "Do my nose and brows and ears. Do it all." Another customer pointed to below the belt. "Do it down there too."

"I'm giving up my car soon," said one of the men ahead of us. Stockinged toes showed through where the tips of his shoes were worn away. "All I use it for is to go out to eat, and I'm too fat." He did not want to move out of the neighborhood. "What do the suburbs got that you can't get right here? You can't escape the crime."

The next customer was a man still working. After my father, he was the saddest one there. "Sam, give me a Russian cut the way Joe Stalin had." A key chain dangled from a belt loop on his jeans. "Make me look like Clark Gable."

He didn't have many jokes to tell. "Keep it short, Sam, I don't know what they'll do." The doctors had found a problem with his prostate. "They asked me if I had any pain, I said, 'No, no pain or blood.' But my job has insurance, and that's good." When Sam finished, the man looked at himself in the mirror. "Just like Gable," he declared without conviction. "Where are the girls?"

My father didn't want to use his walker, so we did those two steps into the chair together. I gave him a boost. He was now too hard of hearing to engage in small talk. "There, you're as good as new," Sam said after five minutes' work. From your lips to God's ears, I thought. It was our last visit.

In August, after sixteen months, Ona left us. Immigration could not deport the spouse of an American citizen; she had found someone to marry in the spring. With a new job lined up, she no longer needed her husband to pick her up for two hours of "shopping" every other day. But she made sure to leave us with options, and she knew we would listen. Only later did we learn Ona had sold the position to a friend.

Marija came to us from New York City, where her last job had died. She is a large woman who speaks English rather poorly, as either a third or fourth language after her native Lithuanian and Polish. I watched her once in the hospital with my mother. She had taken the bus down Kedzie and then walked through Marquette Park to Holy Cross. Either she did not care or understand when we told her how dangerous it was to do that by herself.

A nurse's aide walked into the room. Marija stared at her a moment before saying something in Polish. The woman shook her head, no. But they were able to get by in Ukrainian. Our new housekeeper says, "Very very thanks" or "beauty nice," and we manage, though I am sure she finds our language skills to be woefully deficient.

Marija is a diligent caregiver who makes detailed notes and lists each of her responsibilities on pieces of paper; the kitchen and dining room tables are littered with them. She does not believe that Jerry Springer could make a living on TV in Lithuania. The Baltics are too virtuous for the likes of him. When my father died, she sat in the room praying until the undertakers came for the body. She got his bed sores to heal with a salve from Russia.

My mother did not like her at first; Marija lacked Ona's sense of style. Marija was also attuned to the needs of the household as she found them. My father obviously required a good deal of attention. My mother felt she did as well. It was too hard for her to go back to dressing herself, which Marija found out before long.

Barbara and I have come to depend on her more than we ever did Ona, who made it clear to us that caring for our parents was an ever-greater burden. She did not think of herself as a member of the family and was amused by Barbara's attempts to treat her like one. Marija is more polite when the line between worker and employer grows blurred. She knows it is an occupational hazard.

*A*s their children, we have tried to do right for our parents, to preserve at least some of the dignity to which they were entitled. Heroic gestures have mattered less than maintaining the everyday and familiar. Betty made regular visits just as she had in the first years after moving away while Barbara stocked the refrigerator and cabinets with all the family comfort foods. We also kept taking them to church and dinner. But this routine would have been impossible to maintain without help from our spouses.

Wedding vows recited in youth entail all sorts of commitments that come due one day in middle age. This is what happened to my brother-in-law and wife. Bill often visited after office hours to treat the feet of people he had known for close to forty years, and he sat with them at St. Gall; Barbara either worked or sought time alone. At the restaurant my mother had reached a point where she could not leave before going to the bathroom first. Bill had little choice but to tip the waitress to go in with her.

Other times the job fell to Michele, who struggled to keep her mother-in-law from falling in the stall. There and back my mother was likely to talk about fashion and flowers or trade secrets on child care; she barely noticed the awkwardness of needing help to the toilet. Her attendant had long since become a confidant. So my mother cried about the turn in her husband's temper, and Michele listened. As one woman grew worse, the other could not help but grow sad.

At restaurants my father felt that same urge to visit the restroom after eating. He had to maneuver his walker across the length of a dining room filled with tables and suddenly moving chairs; nor did the bathroom door yield without a firm push. I let him go on his own until he started coming back with urine stains down his pant leg. Then we went together.

I took them on our annual drive to see the fall colors the last Sunday in September. It could have passed for Indian Summer, warm and cloudless, though the trees were still mostly green; waiting did not seem like a good idea. After a half-hour or so, I found a place for brunch. The decor was all red leather and carpeting, a sign of class for people of a certain age. My father said he wanted to go to the bathroom before sitting down.

I shut the door before unzipping his pants. He was still having trouble, so I started to pull down his underwear. He could not stop himself from urinating into my hand. I gagged quietly so as not to draw attention. When we got back to the table, I excused myself to clean up. I returned to find my father ordering an old-fashioned. He and Clare were trying to see who could eat more bread sticks.

All that afternoon in the car Clare and I played a game of Slug-Bug. Whoever was first to see a Volkswagen Beetle slapped the other person while shouting "Slug-Bug, no tag backs, Slug-Bug shield blue," or whatever color it happened to be; there was also the matter of touching hand to foot after a kiss of the fingers, which I found hard to do while driving. Our game of punch and chant amused my mother without violating my father's sense of front-seat decorum. Everyone had such a good time my parents said they wanted to do it again, soon.

The accident in the bathroom bothered me no more than having to take my father to see yet another doctor. Somehow his eyelashes were inverting, a condition that led to scratched corneas. We visited a specialist who prescribed an ointment. I handled this and every other development without comment or complaint. It was my sin to keep so absolutely quiet. I wanted to be just another person waiting to pick up his child in front of school at three o'clock. A dying parent was nobody's business but my own. I prided myself in being able to compartmentalize everything. Keeping secrets was the key. But there came to be too many, and I didn't know how to share.

On Clare's first day off school in October, I drove up north to the old municipal tuberculosis sanitarium, which had been turned into a park complex. In the time before drugs alone dictated the course of treatment, nature was prescribed as part of the cure for disease. So in the early 1920s a young woman sought to recover her health amidst the trees and flowers of a place far from her home on the South Side. Clare and I had a good time that day walking the paths. My mother said she could not recall visiting her sister Lou there.

The next week a radio station asked to interview me on a proposed Chicago landmark. The reporter thought it would be amusing to have a White Sox fan comment on the fate of Wrigley Field. He seemed surprised to hear that the same architect had also designed the original Comiskey Park. We spent part of an afternoon in late October talking while Clare ran up and down the aisles to chase after the ghost of foul balls. Then, before anyone thought to look, it had grown too dark to see what colors favor ivy once a season ends. When I related our adventure, my father hardly seemed to hear. He was too busy trying not to die.

Two days before Halloween my mother passed out at the kitchen table during lunch; Cliff, their neighbor from across the alley, called an ambulance. My mother was waiting for me in the emergency room at Holy Cross. We talked a while, and I began wondering how long it would be for a bed. Sitting next to her, I felt different than the other times there. The possibility that death would choose our cubicle or the next one no longer frightened me. Now I just wanted to be finished and go home. More of the watertight compartments on the *Titanic* were failing.

Those six months between hospital stays showed the extent of my mother's decline. She was now afraid to be alone, and she had none of her earlier confidence about being released. But the miracle of the night-light showed her that God still cared.

Both my parents cast their vote by absentee ballot for Al Gore, after which my father took to his bed. He slept most of the day and whatever he could at night. The state of politics interested him just enough that he asked me from bed during a visit, "Do we have a president yet?" We walked into the bathroom together. In the end, I was wrong to worry about Alzheimer's.

Clare's birthday party fell on a Saturday, so I helped Betty take him and my mother to church. I did not know a person could move as slow as my father did that night without collapsing. At the party he sat on our couch, his face a sickly white from all that had befallen him. He barely spoke to anyone.

On Monday Betty visited him before flying back to Houston. He had fallen down and begun to cry. She asked if he wanted to go to the hospital. It was a question that drew out the last of his strength, as if squeezed from a tube. No, he told her.

On Thursday it was plain he could not go to my in-laws for Thanksgiving; Marija would watch him. On our way to dinner, when I told my mother he would probably be admitted to Holy Cross, she agreed it was a good idea. He'll lose some weight and exercise, she kept saying. She told everyone at the table that her husband was in the hospital already.

I called in the morning only to find that he thought Matt was going to come over to see him. No, I said, he wants you in the hospital. "If that's what the doctor says." He tried to hold back his tears. He was still crying when I left him in his room at Holy Cross.

His kidneys showed some improvement, but not enough for him to avoid making the next decision—to go on dialysis or die. Matt had told me this was coming the last week of August, on a day I just wanted to pick up a prescription refill. Clare was back in school, and I wondered how warm her second-floor classroom would be without air conditioning.

Bill discussed the situation with him. My brother-in-law called to tell me the decision was to do nothing. He would slip away in the next few days. Three times seven. Then he changed his mind in the morning.

I visited him the day before his release; they had just started therapy. A young woman stopped by to evaluate yet another elderly patient and do some exercises. She helped him take his walker across the length of the room while I followed behind with a chair, in case he fell. "You're doing fine," she said in an encouraging voice. "You're just saying that so I won't stop," he cried. When she left, my father told me about a visit over the weekend. The memory left him sobbing. "Your mother looked like a little old lady." With her babushka—covered in a rain hat—and cane, I could not honestly disagree.

On Sunday I took my wife and daughter downtown to the *Christkindlmarket*, a group of German merchants the city brought to Daley Plaza. Shoppers could enjoy Old World linen and bratwurst around that great gift of the Picasso statue. From there we walked over to Field's and saw the tree that sits in the middle of the Walnut Room each year; it was big in the spirit of our old trees at home. My mother called that evening to tell me how they had fought again sitting on the couch.

My father was having dialysis when I visited the next day, and he had it again on Wednesday. Thursday morning after I dropped Clare off at school, there was a message waiting for me on voice mail: Douglas, I think your father dead.

It took me a half-hour to make the drive to Homan Avenue. I walked in to find Manuel's wife on the couch holding my mother as she cried. The police were required to file a report on any death occurring in a residence. After answering questions to their satisfaction, I went into my parents' bedroom.

Their closet door was closed to keep out the winter chill. I found my father lying on his side of the bed, which was closer to the bathroom. Somewhere a commercial played on television. Young actors laughed and danced across the screen as a body grew cold; perhaps they recited a smart line or two of dialogue for Old Navy or The Gap. How could they have known to do otherwise? I bent down and kissed him on the forehead.

The undertakers employed a stretcher that stood the body upright. Before taking it out they made sure the old woman would not see them. She didn't. My mother sat crying behind a closed door in the kitchen.

Perhaps grief provided the clarity of mind for her to know that Edwin J. Bukowski died as he was born eighty-seven years and four months earlier, with the women around him speaking Polish, or that it was twenty-four years to the day since the passing of Richard J. Daley in 1976. But coincidence did little to ease her loss.

Four people of some note died within two weeks of my father. There was Victor Borge, along with Jason Robards, Ray Walston, and William P. Rogers. Only the comic-musician had lived longer. I never tired of watching Borge for the way he blended vaudeville with Chopin. Robards I once saw in a production of O'Neill's *The Iceman Cometh*, and Walston was that Martian everyone in our house laughed at on Sunday evenings. Rogers made the least impression, the same fate he suffered at the hands of Richard Nixon.

For all my practice, the eulogy could have been stronger. I talked about the smell of Old Spice and how phone conversations from HEmlock 4-5574 usually skipped Hello to start with "Yeah, can you . . . ?" But it was only with words Nelson Algren used to describe his own father that I touched on the essence of mine: "Other men wished secretly to be forever drunken. He wished secretly to be forever fixing."

We buried him two days before Christmas, in a December that had already seen too much snow. I do not recall the smell of cornstarch that morning. We had the lunch across from Resurrection, in a building that had once been a terminal for an interurban line to Utica and Starved Rock. My father said that he often waited there for a train.

*M*y father's death revealed two more secrets. One concerned his neighbor Cliff from across the alley, where the Brinkerhoffs used to live. In the years I devoted to finishing a dissertation, my parents happily baby-sat Cliff's two daughters. The girls were their "honorary grandchildren." I was never around to see them engaged in the occupation of honorary grandparents. Harold Ickes and the like did not allow it.

Cliff often asked my father to help him with the kind of household projects I insisted on doing alone. The relationship appeared to benefit both of them. Cliff had never been close to his own father; the man across the alley did a nice job filling in. By then my father had found the patience to explain himself fully; his neighbor made possible a Silver Age for the workbench in the basement. Sorcerer and apprentice sometimes went out drinking together.

My parents liked to celebrate New Year's Eve with Cliff and his wife Bonnie. I have pictures showing an elderly man dressed as Father Time. He wore a sheet over his clothes showing the year about to end. The Confirmation pose of 1927 yielded to 1992; age gave the face more sadness than it deserved. My parents enjoyed themselves at small gatherings like this. An honorary granddaughter is at his side.

I also found the reason for at least a part of my father's anger. He could not accept his wife's deteriorating mental state. Without him to anchor her, my mother went into an accelerated decline. One Saturday morning in January she called to tell me about her dream from the night before. She had caught me making love on the front porch. "I said you better stop it before anyone saw." My mother could not stop laughing at the thought of me this way.

Six hours later she was in tears because Bill hadn't come yet to pick her up for church. "Can you take me?" she asked without any sense of the time or distance involved. When I said it would be impossible to get there in fifteen minutes, she cried even more. I called the next day to find out that my brother-in-law had been maybe five minutes late. She did not remember calling.

On Palm Sunday we sat together at St. Gall while Michele and Clare went outside to be part of the crowd hailing Christ's entry into

Jerusalem. As the procession reached the front of the church, my mother leaned over to whisper, "Marija hits me, but don't say anything. She's a good cook." I told Barbara, and we spoke to Marija, who denied it. Since there were never any bruises, we took the story as another instance of senile confusion.

My father had vivid, often unpleasant dreams about Elizabeth, who made him feel the approach of death. This went on for several years. My mother has experienced similar dreams: Louise is holding a baby she will not let her touch, "and she wouldn't tell me who it belonged to." Another time, when she was dreaming of a home invasion, my mother pinched patches of skin off her wrist in the struggle to keep robbers from taking her wristwatch. Or she will tell me about seeing part of a baby nailed to a tree. It is a dream, dementia, or a discarded doll that somehow landed in the magnolia bush that Betty planted out front. "Do you remember? It was a gift."

That first spring alone proved difficult. On Mother's Day she told the story of a boy from the old neighborhood who had masturbated in front of her; but he died young, my mother added. The story was repeated four times before I walked into the room and told her to stop.

By now she also had begun calling me on the memory-dial phone. Every conversation was the same. "You have to go to Germany. I'll pay you. We need a new Missy." Her miniature schnauzer was lying under the couch out of sight. For two weeks she called this way three or four times a day, until I convinced Barbara a second time that the combination of sleeping pills and anti-depressants wasn't working.

Although my mother improved with a new drug regimen, her walking grew worse from the arthritis in her knee. Then came the cellulitis and a series of hospital stays. In October Matt said she was close to death, only to reverse himself forty-eight hours later. That was nearly three years ago. Recently she was diagnosed with "pre-terminal breathing patterns," but they went away.

I visit my mother at home once or twice a week and talk to her on the phone every other day or so. What anger and exhaustion I felt just before my father's death are gone now. His passing showed me that everything, even a parent's slow decline, reaches an end. So do the phone calls and doctor's visits, along with the chance to kiss someone goodnight.

The two times my mother came down with C-dif, visitors were required to wear plastic gloves. The problem is the antibiotics used to treat the cellulitis; the medicine creates an imbalance of the bacteria in the stomach, which leads to an infectious diarrhea. So I could not stroke her forehead or hold her hand with my own. We were both punished for no good reason. The blessing is that it went away, and she does not remember the isolation, or my feeding her in bed.

Barbara and I have gotten used to the way things are. The situation is harder on Betty. Each trip home she finds someone different and farther removed from the time before. After the last visit, my mother talked about "the one who lives in Texas. She's so tall she takes after our father." Now a second daughter and baby sister are becoming the same person.

My mother endures what I call a peculiar senility that includes spontaneous singing ("March, March, Dombrowski" is one of several favorites), an interest in parties I am supposed to be throwing, and repeating the last line of what people say to her. Her memories are like cards in a deck; each day she is dealt a new hand. She will forget Ford City only to remember something about her trip to Portugal. Somehow her ninth-grade education has led her to De Paul. "I took accounting and typing" among other imagined subjects.

"Why am I so dumb?" she will ask me sometimes while struggling to recall a detail from her life. Yet, regardless of how confused my mother becomes, she can translate Marija's Polish into English for us, and back. In good weather Marija wheels her to the beauty parlor so she can get her hair done. I have now seen enough to appreciate the notion of good days and bad days as one of the profound truths in human existence.

During a visit my mother may look at me and burst into tears. She does not want to live to be a hundred. Or we will have to deal with bad news, like the death of a bridesmaid from her wedding party. The woman is one of those now-anonymous faces in our pictures. Her husband and my father knew each other from Scouts. Eddie Kunka felt bound by his Scout's oath to report his friend's soda-smuggling venture at Camp MacDonald. My father never held it against him.

Mr. Kunka died just after I was married. His wife Frances mourned for twenty-two years. She sent an Easter card to my mother just before her own death. "I think of you and us both," she wrote, "and I think how quickly time goes by. It's everybody, time goes by and we get older, and life gets a little harder for us because we think of how much better it was when our Eds were with us.

"I feel like I'm lost and don't know which way to turn and we cannot discuss things as we did with our husbands somehow it was a big help. Now I'm alone and no one to understand what's in my heart. That's life. . . ." The ellipsis was hers, along with the ending, "I hope you do well we cannot change it." I read only a few parts of the letter to my mother. She felt bad that Frances needed a pacemaker.

Unlike her husband, my mother does not fear dying. She often cries that people have forgotten her, but she remains convinced God will remember this child as His very good servant. She talks of heaven and how she will look down on Clare. Her theology, if nothing else, remains strong.

*O*ther Baby Boomers would be forever young with an assist from plastic surgery or Botox injections, but wrinkles do not frighten me. Standing alone does. I have always shared the deference some adult children show their parents. Such a person is happiest standing in the shadow of elders. When one or both parents die, that is no longer possible, however much the child keeps trying. "Son of" is a title of surprising comfort.

There are ways to compensate. Two years ago we used the old molds for an Easter Lamb; Michele and Betty baked, I lifted. In the storage box we found an envelope filled with Lamb recipes. There was also a page of notes from the master baker; he recorded the results of each year's efforts over the course of several years. The final entry is from 1990: "I baked large lamb 350 deg. oven, 70 min. Small lamb one hour. I used a half of cup less powdered sugar." We now have something to build on.

Or a memory will lie in wait for me when I help Marija around the house. She worries that "bad boys come in yard." Cutting through gangways is a time-honored tradition on Homan Avenue, though a gate left open could cost my mother and her caregiver their dog. Marija bought a lock at the Dollar Store, but the chain was all wrong. So I went into the garage to find her a better one.

Off in a corner next to the extension ladders was a shelf filled with flags; they are a deluxe version of the kind put on graves for Memorial Day. I counted fourteen, which may have been a magic number for my father. Some are plastic, others cloth, and all of them have gold tips on their staffs. Each flag is bound with paper rings, seven of which have "50 stars" written on them. This could only mean he kept a flag with forty-eight stars. I picked the one on the biggest stick, and that was it. My mother will find her own way of coming to us, maybe with lilacs or hemlines.

I have spent much of my life looking for a community in the spirit of Homan Avenue. The New Urbanism champions the idea of old neighborhoods, just not mine; Carl closed down long ago, and he took his dice with him. I have this picture of Shangri-la laid out on a grid, where the communion of saints will be housed in bungalows. Affection for a place and the certainty of its goodness are the product of a stable childhood, another gift from my parents to their son. How many moves does a family get before their daughter feels otherwise? El Dorados, even of the simplest sort, do not return.

About eight years ago I found a street that felt comfortable, and so we moved there, only to arrive too late. Next door was a massive elm that reached over onto our side. It reminded me of the trees along Homan Avenue before Dutch elm destroyed them. The disease showed its contempt by leaving a line of stumps behind.

Our next-door neighbor had his elm cut down three years ago. He did not see leaves with gently serrated edges or their funny shape, oblong with a point, as if drawn by a child uncertain how to make an oval. No, the leaves were a nuisance to rake, and the roots broke into his sewer line. An old person cannot be expected to love nature as a child does. Heart attacks lurk in every bushel of leaves.

This is not the only change on our street. People from six of the twenty-one houses on either side of Wisconsin Avenue have moved on. They grew old and died or were taken away by relatives in order to prepare. At the end of our block was an old woman without any teeth. On her front door was a sign, God Bless Our Country, and in her backyard a bird bath painted red, white, and blue. Clare was too afraid to take the treat she offered one summer's evening.

The man across the street from her always wore an old work shirt from one of the big factories that has since closed down, and he kept a shopping cart in the backyard. This made for a walker when he wasn't leaning against the fence or on his lawnmower. The two sisters in adjacent bungalows just down from us spent summers sharing a bench on the front porch; they always smiled and waved. The couple across the street did not mind when Clare hit line drives into their bushes. They are all gone now.

The woman living across the alley from us on Wenonah looked to be older than my parents. She spent hours in the yard with her dog. They were both quite small and extremely slow; it was the animal that disappeared first. One afternoon in early spring the woman walked over to our gate and asked if she could talk to our basset hound. A few days later she told me how one morning in December she found her companion lying next to a table with the telephone on it. The dog was dead.

She just had him to the vet and couldn't understand, even if he was seventeen years old. Several weeks later I saw a pile of boxes behind her house. There were all sorts of family pictures in them and a play-bill showing Ray Walston in the touring company of *South Pacific*. Her house had to be emptied of its past. The old neighborhood is dead. Long live our new neighbors.

But I raise our daughter the same way old generals fight the next war, looking backward. No one has ever called me a dumb or dirty Po-lack, yet I act as if it is a common slight. Injuries now three generations old shape the life of our child. I am not interested in seeing all of them healed. She will bring home good grades, and she will keep her face clean. The problem for me is that the Becvars do not live down the block to take Clare in for lunch or keep an eye on her in the alley, and the nuns are unable to dispense any more batting tips.

As a child I was overwhelmed by the likes of State Street, where everyone and everything seemed so alive. I did not care to know what my parents already did. They were to be my buffers against the old age and illness of others. I did not want them to show me how life winds down, but they did. Our daughter has learned this well ahead of me.

We could not pretend to Clare that her grandfather was all right. Lies can be as unsettling as hospital beds. So she went with us to visit. Sitting together on the couch at home, my father and daughter some-times watched magicians perform on television. She liked David

Copperfield, he told her about Houdini. Clare even performed magic in the hospital by making a quarter disappear out of her hand. Grandpa smiled at the trickery mastered by this favorite child of his. It was another miracle.

There are times when the family pictures are a tempting place to hide, provided I edit out the most recent ones of my parents. The Super Paks can make them young again. Only that would deny how my daughter saw her grandparents. And therein lies the last gift Edwin and Mary Ann Bukowski bestowed on their family. They taught us to accept mortality and death.

I struggle with this lesson in a culture that prefers comedy. Rather than cry, it is better to recall Chuckles the Clown—killed by an elephant, laughed over by Mary Richards—or the weekend Hollywood high jinks of two guys and a corpse. More solemn moments are reserved for the sitcom star who collapses on set and expires soon after. But the show must go on. Too much mourning risks doing it to death.

Headstones, though, are still permissible. My father's has a design based on the logo for the Chicago Fire Fighters Union, Local 2; it shows a circle of hose crowned with a fireman's helmet. This is the best way to remember him, I think. The day we shopped for the stone, Barbara treated Clare to lunch. We all sat at the counter so our meals could be delivered on the flatbed cars of a Lionel train.

My parents were fitful visitors to Resurrection; a cemetery is perhaps the most difficult expression of community to accept. It was other people who spent their Sunday afternoons planting graveside flowers or using clippers to cut grass around headstones. My father does not reside at Resurrection, only his body in a casket. I visit probably for the same reason he did—to be humbled and honor the memory of another.

The cemetery office has put grave locations on computer. There are four listings for "Baby Bukowski." The ones from 1907 and 1908 could be my father's siblings; they are buried in a section next to Stanley's. Otherwise my father and the other members of his family appear no closer to one another in death than they were for most of their lives.

The grave is a few yards from the road. For someone who always worried over traffic, this seems fitting. On the way to White Sox games we parked the car at a firehouse just off of 35th Street. Other fans were left to beat the rush. I imagine it will be no different for my father with the Second Coming.

His section of the cemetery is pleasant enough, with a large pine tree nearby; perpetual care may or may not keep the crabgrass from encroaching on the headstone. I like the sound of passing trains and how the steam rises out of the smokestacks at Argo. Resting alongside my father are two veterans of World War II, a seaman second class and private first class. Men of service lie three in a row.

But a grave is not required for memory. Sometimes I recall how I made my father laugh, which had little to do with a shared sense of humor. Five minutes of watching me watch Monty Python convinced him, "Anyone who likes this has taste for shit." Rather, he smiled when I gave voice to his feelings. It happened twice that I know of after hospital stays.

Following his initial release, a Canadian television company hired me as an adviser for a crime documentary about Leopold and Loeb. My job basically consisted of looking at a list of possible locations to say that nearly everything had been lost during Hyde Park's embrace of urban renewal. Or I questioned how they could shoot film of buildings that did not exist at the time of Bobby Franks's murder in 1924. The ways of television are not my ways.

At the end of a week I got paid in cash. "There I was standing on East 47th Street with five hundred-dollar bills," I related during a visit to my parents. "I kept wondering, 'What if the police stop me? How do I convince them I'm not looking for drugs?'" And he smiled, the way he did seven months later when I told him about my adventures in plumbing with a clogged basement drain. "I asked myself, 'What would Ed Bukowski do?'"

The cold and the tears relented just long enough for him to answer with a grin, "Swear a lot."

I also remember another Sunday afternoon in early autumn when my father's recovery still seemed possible. Michele and I celebrated by taking Clare to Kiddieland, an old amusement park with wooden pavilions and space for Skee Ball. A wish comes true for every ball that finds the 50-point hole. Or maybe that was the arcade at Riverview.

Clare wanted to ride the Ferris wheel, and I drew the short straw. We sat together, parent and child, going up and around in a gondola that had seen it all a million times before. Ahead of us rose DuPage County, an affluent mirage in my life and now our daughter's. Far to the left were St. Laurence, Resurrection, and a string of suburbs where my classmates had moved to raise families and their grown-up children were leaving for points more distant. Too many memories can leave a person dizzy. There were other places for us to go that day.

I do make an effort to live in the present. For those other times there are the Super Paks or the Faith and Freedom readers I now collect; my mother relied on the adventures of David and Ann in teaching me to read. Which book she used I can't say for sure. Those evenings spent in the kitchen forty-six years ago come with less clarity than I would like, and the original was thrown out as clutter.

If I had to choose one, it would be *This Is Our Family*, copyright 1942 by Ginn and Company. The cover shows David and Ann playing with Baby Mary in her buggy. Behind them is a bungalow. The illustration on the last page shows their home beneath a starry sky. "God looked down on three happy children," that last page reads. "He looked down on a good father and mother. He loved them. He blessed them."

All our pictures said so.

Memory is a tricky thing best approached with the aid of scholarship. The following works helped me remember the summer of 1966 while assessing the issue of race in Chicago: Arnold R. Hirsch, *Making the Second Ghetto: Race and Housing in Chicago, 1940–1960*; Sanford D. Horwitt, *Let Them Call Me Rebel: Saul Alinsky—His Life and Legacy*; Harold M. Mayer and Richard C. Wade, *Chicago: Growth of a Metropolis*; and James R. Ralph, Jr., *Northern Protest: Martin Luther King Jr., Chicago, and the Civil Rights Movement*. In addition, Alan Ehrenhalt's *The Lost City: Discovering the Forgotten Virtues of Community in the Chicago of the 1950s* highlighted the sublime and the tragic—Talman and Alvin Palmer—while three newspapers in particular covered the news of those ninety days from the vantage point of faith, neighborhood, and downtown, respectively. Like the rest of us that summer, the *New World*, the *Southwest News-Herald*, and the *Sun-Times* struggled to make sense of events that demanded attention.

Other works I have noted include Edith Abbott, *The Tenements of Chicago, 1908–1935*; Jane Addams, *Twenty Years at Hull-House*; Nelson Algren, "Everything Inside Is a Penny," in *The Last Carousel*; Eldridge Cleaver, *Soul on Ice*; William Cronon, *Nature's Metropolis: Chicago and the Great West*; Judith Mara Gutman, *Lewis W. Hine and the American Social Conscience*; Lewis W. Hine (with an Introduction by Freddy Langer), *The Empire State Building*; Langston Hughes, *The Big Sea*; A. J. Liebling, *Chicago: The Second City*; Glen E. Holt and Dominic Pacyga, *Chicago: A Historical Guide to the Neighborhoods, The Loop and South Side*; Mike Royko, *Boss*; Carl Sandburg, *Chicago Poems*; Henry David Thoreau, *Walden*; Frederic M. Thrasher (with an editor's preface by Robert E. Park), *The Gang: A Study of 1,313 Gangs in Chicago*; and Louise Carroll Wade, *Chicago's Pride: The Stockyards, Packingtown, and Environs in the Nineteenth Century*.

A NOTE ON THE AUTHOR

Douglas Bukowski was born in Chicago, grew up on the South Side, and studied at De Paul University and the University of Illinois at Chicago, where he received a Ph.D. in American history and later taught. Mr. Bukowski has written for several Chicago publications and is the author of *Big Bill Thompson, Chicago, and the Politics of Image*; *Navy Pier: A Chicago Landmark*; and *Baseball Palace of the World: The Last Year of Comiskey Park*. He lives in Berwyn, Illinois, with his wife and daughter.